Cicerone County Walking Series

WALKING
IN
HAMPSHIRE

ABOUT THE AUTHORS

Nick Channer has written over 20 walking and travel guides, including *Untrodden Ways*, a guide to Britain's lesser-known long-distance footpaths. He has written several books on Hampshire, and regularly writes about the county in the 'Down Your Way' section of *Country Walking* magazine. He has explored much of Hampshire on foot, and his travels were regularly broadcast on BBC Radio Solent's weekday afternoon show for several years.

David Foster has lived and walked in Hampshire since 1987. He is an accomplished freelance writer, with a lively, knowledgeable style that reflects a lifelong enthusiasm for the countryside. He has worked for the *Times*, the *Independent* and the *Express*, as well as for magazines including *Country Walking*. He is a member of the Outdoor Writers' Guild.

Cicerone County Walking Series

Walking in Bedfordshire	*Alan Castle*
Walking in Berkshire	*Robert Wilson*
Walking in Buckinghamshire	*Robert Wilson*
Walking in Cheshire	*Carl Rogers*
Walking in Cornwall	*John Earle*
Walking in County Durham	*Paddy Dillon*
Walking in Devon	*David Woodthorpe*
Walking in Dorset	*James Roberts*
Walking in Kent, vols 1 and 2	*Kev Reynolds*
Walking in Lancashire	*Mary Welsh*
Walking in Northumberland	*Alan Hall*
Walking in Oxfordshire	*Leslie Tomlinson*
Walking in Somerset	*James Roberts*
Walking in Staffordshire	*Julie Meech*
Walking in Sussex	*Kev Reynolds*
Walking in Warwickshire	*Brian Conduit*
Walking in Worcestershire	*David Hunter*

Cicerone County Walking Series

WALKING
IN
HAMPSHIRE

by

Nick Channer
and
David Foster

Cp

CICERONE PRESS
2 POLICE SQUARE, MILNTHORPE, LA7 7PY
www.cicerone.co.uk

© Nick Channer & David Foster 2001
ISBN 1 85284 311 X
A catalogue record for this book is available from the British Library.

Acknowledgements

Much of the research for this book was carried out with patient help from staff in the Reference and Local Studies sections at Winchester Public Library. Hampshire County Council's Rights of Way section has been a valuable source of advice over many years and, in particular, Marilyn Meeks provided much of the material about long distance paths. The cricket historian James Coldham advised on the game's Hampshire origins. Finally, grateful thanks to Stephen Jenkinson of the Institute of Public Rights of Way Officers for his help with the section on pathway law.

David Foster
Nick Channer

Contents

INTRODUCTION 9
County history 9
Hampshire's wildlife 12
Pathway law..13
What to take with you 15
How to use this book..16

THE WALKS

1   Remains of a Royal Forest: Mottisfont and West Tytherley 18

2   The Silk Route: Whitchurch...25

3   Cobbett Country: Hurstbourne Tarrant...............................30

4   Discovering Danebury Ring: Stockbridge 35

5   By the Basingstoke Canal: Odiham 41

6   A Walk on Watership Down: Kingsclere 46

7   The Portals' Paper Chase: Whitchurch and Overton 51

8   Hiking to Hannington: Overton and Hannington....................55

9   Hampshire Heartlands: The Candover Valley 60

10 Silchester Roman Town: Bramley and Silchester......................65

11 Border Country: Petersfield 70

12 War and Peace: The Meon Valley..76

13 The American Connection: West Meon....................................82

14 Gilbert White's Outdoor Laboratory: Selborne 87

15 In Search of Sheep Droves: Bentworth 93

16 Buckland Rings: Lymington 96

17 Coasting Along: Lymington and the Solent.............................100

18 Hampshire's Amazing Mizmaze: Whitsbury Village 103

19 Castleman's Corkscrew: Through the New Forest 108
from Ashurst to Brockenhurst

20 Exploring Conan Doyle Country: Lyndhurst and Minstead 114

21 Gateway to the World: Southampton 120

22 'Pompey': Britain's Island City: Portsmouth 126

23 Sea Breezes: Titchfield and Fareham 132

24 Forest of Bere: Wickham and Soberton Heath 136

25 The Itchen Navigation: Winchester to Eastleigh 140

26 Kingsley's Walk: Micheldever Wood 146

27 On the Dole: New Alresford 150

28 Along the Itchen Valley: North of Winchester 156

29 Waller's Walk: Kings Worthy 164

30 Sauntering around Sparsholt: Sparsholt and 168
Farley Mount Country Park

31 Ghost Trains and German Bombers: Horsebridge 172
and King's Somborne

32 A Hurricane Walk: South-east from Winchester 177

Long Distance Paths 183

Bibliography 186

KEY TO MAPS

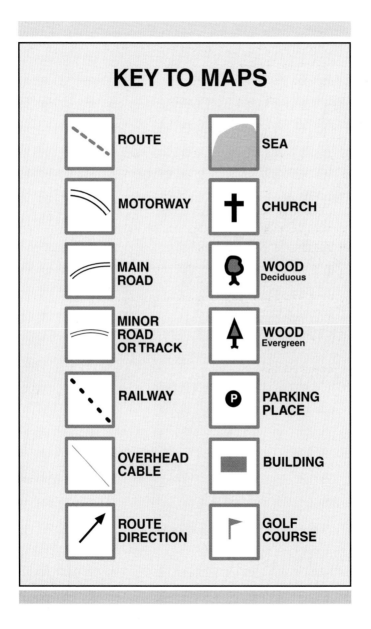

ROUTE

SEA

MOTORWAY

CHURCH

MAIN ROAD

WOOD Deciduous

MINOR ROAD OR TRACK

WOOD Evergreen

RAILWAY

PARKING PLACE

OVERHEAD CABLE

BUILDING

ROUTE DIRECTION

GOLF COURSE

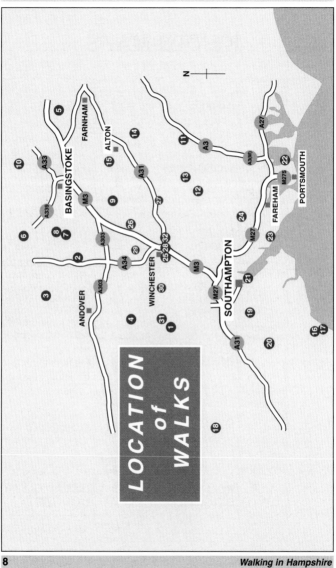

Introduction

Why walk? It seems a fair question for, as society becomes ever more mobile, few people actually need to walk anywhere at all.

Yet walking remains immensely popular. Between us, we take over a third of a billion country walks in England and Wales every year – and with good reason. For walking offers escape from the pressures of everyday life; the motorway, the internet and the shopping mall. It imposes a rhythm of its own.

A solitary walk can be a liberating experience, offering freedom, independence and a chance for some quiet reflection. With family or friends, walking becomes more companionable; an opportunity for conversation and shared experience.

Besides being one of the easiest ways of getting out and about in the countryside, walking is the perfect partner to a whole range of interests from birdwatching and brewing to literature and local history. It's an enjoyable way of keeping fit, with the added incentive of a quiet drink or a meal at a wayside inn.

This book contains a varied selection of walks from across the length and breadth of Hampshire. Each route is described in detail, and highlights some of the main points of interest along the way. If you're new to walking, the sections on equipment and pathway law will help to get you started – and, we hope, encourage you to discover more of Hampshire's 3000 miles of pathways for yourself.

But, as an appetizer, let's start with a review of Hampshire's history and wildlife.

County history

To discover Hampshire's past you would need to embark on a journey to the very heart of the county. Along the way the search would yield evidence of Hampshire's early history, how it was influenced by the Roman occupation and how its coastline defended this country against attack over the years. And much more besides would be unearthed in your progress through the centuries.

INTRODUCTION

The county's name was first recorded in AD757, as Hamtunscir – 'the shire of Hamtun'. Hamtun is the old name for Southampton, in the days when it was a walled town. In fact, for many years Hampshire's official name was 'The County of Southampton'. Southampton later gained a reputation as one of the world's leading ports, playing host to the greatest liners.

More than 450 scheduled ancient monuments lie within Hampshire's boundaries, giving a fascinating insight into the county's long and complex history. Bronze Age round barrows litter the landscape, and from the seventh century BC onwards Iron Age tribes built the great hill forts, the remains of which can still be seen in places today. Old Winchester Hill and Danebury Hill are among the most notable examples. Following the Roman invasion, this part of southern England was swallowed by Alfred's kingdom of Wessex.

Below the old hill forts, close to the Solent, lies the New Forest, the jewel in Hampshire's crown. The largest remaining unspoilt medieval forest in Western Europe and once a royal preserve, it is a romantic place of dark legends and historic literary associations. The forest, extending roughly from the south coast to the Wiltshire border, conjures up images of wild, uncultivated tracts of land and extensive dense woodland. In medieval times that is precisely how the region was made up. Today, apart from obvious signs of commercialism, the New Forest has changed little since William the Conqueror established it as his deer park.

From this vast, wooded landscape your journey of discovery would surely take you to Winchester, at the heart of Hampshire and once the capital of England. No visit to the county is complete without a tour of this most historic of English cities. Winchester was an important centre from Roman times when it was known as Venta Belgarum. Later, it became the capital of England and Wessex under the Anglo-Saxons. William the Conqueror retained Winchester as his capital and built a castle here, though much of it was destroyed during the Civil War.

That great conflict of the seventeenth century left its mark on Hampshire. The ruins of Basing House and the blood-stained battle-field at Cheriton, among other sites, are a permanent reminder of the bitter struggle for power and supremacy.

The Tudor House, Southampton (Walk 20)

The 350 or so years since the Civil War have witnessed the most significant developments and the greatest upheaval in the county's history. The eighteenth and nineteenth centuries saw major changes in agriculture, the dawn of the transport age and the coming of the Industrial Revolution. The last century watched Hampshire's urban areas grow as never before and now there is little to separate Southampton and Winchester or Fareham and Portsmouth.

It may be increasingly difficult to escape encroaching urbanisation and intrusive reminders of the modern world, but a forest walk or a riverside stroll does transport us 'far from the madding crowd' to a rustic, rural haven where, albeit briefly, you can wallow in the peace and quiet of the countryside. With its charming villages, rolling farmland, scenic forests and gentle river valleys, Hampshire is blessed with some of the finest walking country in the south of England – criss-crossed by a network of ancient paths and tracks which evolved over the years as a vital means of communication. Different generations used these routes as they went to work in the fields and factories, or travelled to school, market or church, and to surrounding towns and villages. Each path has its own story to tell, reflecting the countryside's many social and economic changes. And by exploring these primitive routes today, you are quite literally walking over Hampshire's history.

Hampshire's wildlife

Think of Hampshire and you think, perhaps, of the rolling chalk downlands that comprise some forty per cent of the county. The North and South Downs both have their roots in east Hampshire, buttressing the Hampshire Downs to the north and west of Winchester.

Here lie sweeping expanses of arable farmland. All year round larks and kestrels hover in the wide skies, whilst pheasant or partridge forage on the ground below. In late spring, swifts and swallows arrive from Africa to pass their summer hunting insects over the cornfields. Most of the terrestrial wildlife is confined to hedgerows and field edges and, by late summer, plants like willow-herb, knapweed and red campion will be brushing the walkers' clothing. The county is home to more than forty species of butterfly, and even untrained eyes will easily spot orange tips, peacocks and red admirals.

At the foot of the downs, two of England's most famous chalk streams – the Test and the Itchen – flow lazily through luxuriant water meadows. Before the Second World War many of these meadows were flooded each winter to improve the spring grazing, and much of their present fertility stems from this custom. Naturalists catalogue unusual grasses such as red fescue or Yorkshire fog, but colourful wildflowers like ragged robin, comfrey and orange balsam are more obvious to most of us. The fens are home to both reed and sedge warblers, whilst coot, moorhen, dabchick and Canada geese live on the rivers.

Around the time of the Norman conquest much of southern England was thickly wooded and, even today, Hampshire is well endowed with ancient, semi-natural woodland. Besides the ubiquitous beech trees you'll find hazel, oak, maple and hawthorn, to name but a few. Animals, too, live in the woods: squirrels, stoats, hares, foxes and deer. In springtime, bluebells garnish the woodland floor and species such as primrose, stitchwort, bugle and wild violet also thrive in the dappled shade. In fact the great joy of these ancient woodlands is their sheer variety; an English oak, for instance, supports over 280 different species of insect.

No outline of the county's wildlife would be complete without mention of the great glory of south-west Hampshire. The New Forest is neither new, nor does it conform to most people's idea of a forest. However, it remains the largest area of uncultivated land in lowland England and is internationally important for its abundance of rare plants, insects and birds. The 9000 acres of 'ancient and ornamental' woodlands are possibly the least altered remnants of the primeval wildwood that covered southern Britain after the close of the last Ice Age. Yet, for the average visitor, the joy of the New Forest lies not in its scientific significance but in the tranquillity of its woodland glades and the charm of its ponies grazing peacefully on vast, unenclosed heaths.

Only a small fraction of all this natural profusion is visible from the road. To see it all would take a lifetime of patient study; but you can make a start by leaving the car in the garage, pocketing your map, and setting off down quiet pathways on your feet.

Pathway law

As soon as you leave your own front gate, you enter someone else's property. Because most of us step directly onto a road or other public land, we scarcely give it a moment's thought; but straight away, our legal status has changed.

Many people worry about leaving the familiar road, and setting out on a path across someone else's land. Yet that's not such a big step as leaving home in the first place, for the road and the path are both public highways. So just what is the law, and what can you do if things go wrong?

A public right of way is simply a legal right to go to and fro along defined routes without trespassing. You can stop along the way for refreshment, and you may also take your dog with you. But never – ever – allow him off the lead near livestock or through farmyards. Dogs are a potential hazard to all farm animals, and a farmer is legally entitled to shoot a dog found worrying his stock.

In law, there are three kinds of path: *footpath*, *bridleway* and *byway*. Footpaths may only be used on foot, and bridleways are for walkers, horseriders and cyclists. Normally, it is a criminal offence to use an unauthorised motorbike or car on these paths. *Byways open to all traffic* are public roads that are used mainly as footpaths or bridleways. You may still see *roads used as public paths* marked on some maps. The legal position of these roads is currently being reviewed, but walkers are still entitled to use them.

A legal right isn't much use if you don't know that you've got it. So County Councils must, by law, keep an up-to-date *definitive map* showing the paths in their areas. These maps are available for the public to see, and are the source of rights of way information on Ordnance Survey maps.

Country paths are highways in the same way as public roads. The County Council has a duty to maintain and signpost them, although they aren't required to make up the surface of byways for motor traffic. Where small obstructions like brambles or a fallen branch block your path, you may remove as little as necessary to clear a way through. And, speaking of obstructions, the general rule is that an adult bull must not be kept on his own in a field with a path running through it.

Farmers may plough up the surface of cross-field paths to grow crops, but paths which skirt field edges must not be ploughed at any time. When paths are ploughed, the farmer must restore the surface afterwards, and make sure that the route can still be seen clearly through any growing crops. Usually this restoration must be done within two weeks of disturbing the path.

County Councils have various powers to close or divert public paths. They can also make orders affecting the actual use of a path, for instance by prohibiting motor traffic on byways or roads used as public paths. Minor changes are made to the pathway network from time to time, so it pays to have an up-to-date map, and to be polite and co-operative on the very rare occasions when problems arise on the ground.

Finally, if you should encounter a problem on your walk, keep a note of the exact location and report it to the highway authority. In most of Hampshire this is the County Council but, in Portsmouth and Southampton, you'll need to contact the relevant City Council.

Their addresses are shown below:

Hampshire County Council,
Arts, Countryside and Community Dept,
Mottisfont Court, High Street, Winchester, Hampshire SO23 8ZF
Tel: 01962 846045

Portsmouth City Council,
Highways Management Section, Engineering & Design Service,
Civic Offices, Guildhall Square, Portsmouth PO1 2AS
Tel: 0800 216815

Southampton City Council,
Rights of Way Officer,
Civic Centre, Civic Centre Road, Southampton SO14 7LS
Tel: 023 8083 3987

What to take with you

The beauty of walking is its simplicity; you can complete any of the walks in this book without spending a fortune on equipment and special clothing. But a few simple preparations will help to make your walks more enjoyable.

At all costs, look after your feet. In hot, dry weather, you can trot along quite happily in light cotton socks and a good pair of trainers. Remember, though, that country paths take a week or more to dry out after rain; then, you'll be grateful for some thick woollen socks and a decent pair of waterproof boots.

Clothing should be comfortable, too. The secret is to wear as little as possible without getting chilly, so it's usually better to have several thin layers that you can put on or take off at will. Even in summer the weather can quickly turn wet, so carry a light waterproof jacket that rolls up small when you don't need it.

Do take a decent map; the Ordnance Survey's new *Explorer* and *Outdoor Leisure* series are particularly good. Besides giving you a complete picture of the local landscape, your map will get you back on course if you're unlucky enough to stray off-route. Fold the map to show the right area and protect it with a clear polythene bag, or with one of the inexpensive map cases available from most outdoor shops.

You'll see a lot more wildlife than you do from your car, so a comprehensive field guide such as Paul Sterry's *Complete British Wildlife* (HarperCollins) is a worthwhile investment. A pocket-sized pair of binoculars will bring birds and animals closer still – and they're also useful for picking out distant landmarks. On the same subject, don't forget a little something to eat and drink. It makes stopping to look at the view far more rewarding!

So there you are. A spare jumper, your waterproof, the map in its case. Field guide, binoculars and some light refreshment – is that it? Well, not quite. The camera and first aid kit always seem to be forgotten until the moment they're needed. You, of course, will be better prepared...

Lastly, you'll want a small rucksack of around thirty litres capacity, to shoulder your bits and pieces in comfort. Get one with some outside pockets, to help keep track of all those odds and ends that will otherwise lurk at the bottom of the bag when you want them.

How to use this book

Many people plan a walk in the countryside simply by plotting a route on the Ordnance Survey map. A simple enough idea. But how can you be sure that the walk will be an enjoyable one?

For example, what do you know of the route and what might you expect of the scenery or the local attractions? How can you find out if there is a good picnic site en route or a welcoming pub at the end of the walk? Who can help you with general information on the area and how well is it served by public transport?

A good walk poses many questions but, without a comprehensive guidebook, you don't have all the answers. As well as recording vitally important route-finding instructions, a reputable walking guide should contain everything you need to know about the walk. It should even include a basic sketch map, though the relevant Ordnance Survey map is also recommended to help navigate your way round the more complex parts of the route.

In order to help you gain some idea of what to expect from these Hampshire walks, each of the 32 routes begins with a few brief details about the length of the walk, where it starts and finishes and where you may find suitable refreshment. Terrain is covered too, as the likely conditions of the walk need to be carefully considered. Among other factors, this helps you to decide on the type of footwear to take. Remember that public rights of way can change almost beyond recognition during the year. What might be an easy ramble in summer, with the ground firm and dry as a bone underfoot, can turn into an arduous trek along waterlogged bridleways and slippery paths in winter. Woodland and forest walks are notoriously wet in places for many months of the year. The time allowed for each walk is difficult to estimate but two to three miles an hour is about average. Allow longer if the ground is very wet or if making any detours along the way.

The telephone numbers of local tourist information centres, stately homes open to the public and local visitor centres are listed to help you obtain useful information about what to see and do in the county. In the summer months, it is very pleasant to spend half the day on an enjoyable walk, stop for lunch afterwards at a local inn and then perhaps round off the trip with a visit to a local National Trust house or a museum.

How to get to and from the start of the walk is also very important. All but a handful of the walks are served by public transport, but if a car is your preference, then details of where to park are listed. Twenty-eight of the described walks are circular, while four are linear. With these, it is often easier to drive to the finish of the walk first and then take the train to where the route starts.

Hampshire County Council produces a comprehensive map of bus, rail and ferry services in the county, listing all transport operators. Write to:

Hampshire County Council
Passenger Transport Group
The Castle
Winchester
Hampshire
SO23 8UD

For up-to-date train times, contact the National Rail Enquiry Line on 08457 484950.

Walk 1 – Remains of a Royal Forest

Mottisfont and West Tytherley

Distance:	13 miles
Start/Finish:	Mottisfont village. There is a railway station at Dunbridge about half a mile from the start of the walk.
Terrain:	Country roads, field paths and tracks, stretches of woodland and parkland, byways and bridleways. Sections of the walk can be extremely wet in mid-winter.
Parking:	Limited spaces outside Mottisfont Church
Map:	OS Landranger sheet 184 OS Landranger sheet 185 OS Explorer sheet 131
Refreshments:	The Black Horse, West Tytherley The Star, East Tytherley Teas and morning coffee served at Mottisfont Post Office Licensed restaurant at Mottisfont Abbey Visitors to St Andrew's Church at Mottisfont are welcome to picnic in the churchyard.
Information:	Tourist Information Centre: 01794 512987 (closed in winter) Mottisfont Abbey: 01794 340757

One of Hampshire's most closely guarded secrets is revealed on this splendid border walk in the west of the county. Straddling the Hampshire/Wiltshire boundary, this is perfect walking country, a veritable treasure trove of rural delights. And yet it remains largely undiscovered. Go there at any time of the year and thankfully we will have much of it to ourselves.

It is here, at the very heart of the countryside, that we can trace the remains of an ancient forest, an even greater secret among Hampshire's hidden gems. The old Royal Forest of Buckholt has all but disappeared; however, pockets of woodland remain and there is still a small settlement known as Buckholt – the name possibly means beechwood.

Before beginning the walk have a look at **Mottisfont**'s twelfth-century Grade I listed church which contains explanatory boards in several languages. From the centre of the village, part of the Mottisfont estate, walk up the road beside the tithe barn, following it round to the right. We are currently on the Test Way, heading along Oakley Road. Glancing to the right reveals very pleasant views across the Test Valley. At the point where the Test Way leaves the road and heads across the fields, we can pause and lean on the gate to peer at nearby **Mottisfont Abbey** and its surroundings.

The National Trust property was originally a twelfth-century Augustinian priory, before becoming a private house after the Dissolution. The abbey includes a drawing room decorated by Rex Whistler and a superb walled garden containing one of the finest collections of roses in the country. A tributary of the nearby Test flows through the elegant grounds and the abbey is known for the spring or 'font' from which its name is derived. Mottisfont Abbey and gardens are open to the public during the summer months.

Avoid a lane on the right and take the next left turning. Pass Great Copse and continue through the trees to the road junction. Bear right and walk down to Hillside Cottage on the left. Veer right in front of it to a stile. Head diagonally across the field to a stile in the far corner, cross a stream and hug the tongue of woodland on the right. Go straight across the field towards the buildings of Bentley Farms where we join a lane and pass the entrance to Little Bentley Farm. On reaching a fork, by some double gates, keep right. Follow the track to a T junction, crossing over to pick our way between the trees. Pheasants may suddenly burst from the undergrowth here, retreating into the skies to the sound of our approaching footsteps. In places, our path is strewn with the debris of fallen branches and ancient tree roots, reaching out across the ground like some haphazard obstacle course.

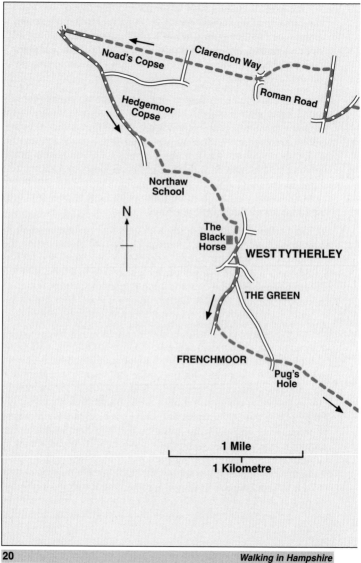

Noad's Copse

Clarendon Way

Roman Road

Hedgemoor Copse

Northaw School

N

The Black Horse

WEST TYTHERLEY

THE GREEN

FRENCHMOOR

Pug's Hole

1 Mile

1 Kilometre

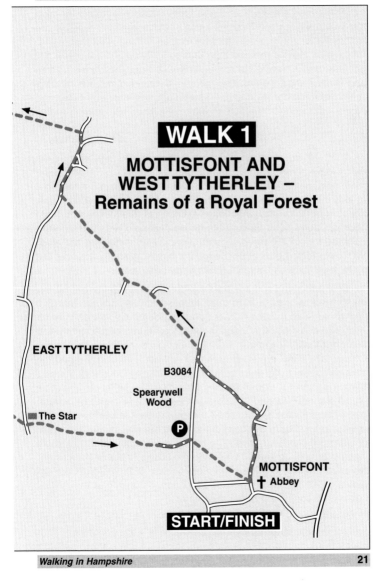

WALK 1

**MOTTISFONT AND
WEST TYTHERLEY –
Remains of a Royal Forest**

EAST TYTHERLEY

B3084

Spearywell
Wood

The Star

P

MOTTISFONT
✝ Abbey

START/FINISH

At the road turn right and pass Queenwood Farm. Take the next turning on the left and bear left again at the crossroads. Now we are following the route of an old **Roman road** linking Winchester with Old Sarum. Pass a farm and then look to the horizon for a seemingly endless row of trees etched against the skyline. The bare branches and lengthening shadows lend the curtain of woodland a noticeably stark quality on dark winter days. Eventually our route curves left and passes beneath the branches of some yew trees, so common to this part of the county. Turn right by a 'National Byway' sign and follow the byway for about half a mile to the route of the **Clarendon Way**.

Turn left and head towards Buckholt Farm. On approaching the farm outbuildings, we veer left to skirt them. Go straight on at the road, pass a pair of cottages on the right and cross the next road to a muddy track, a continuation of the Roman road and Clarendon Way. Keep on the track and eventually we come up to a junction by some houses, one of them bearing the unusual name 'Owl's Castle'. Turn left here to join the footpath, following it up the slope to the road. We have crossed the county boundary into Wiltshire by now but our route soon takes us back into Hampshire once more.

Bear left and eventually pass a turning for West Tytherley; further on we walk alongside farm outbuildings and pig units on the right. Our route takes us ever deeper into this extensively wooded border country where busy roads and the intrusive sounds of the twenty-first century thankfully seem a world away. Follow the road to Pimlico Cottage and then branch off left to join a woodland path. Beyond the trees we follow the defined path to a stile in the far boundary. Looking back, our view is dominated by a vast curtain of trees. Continue ahead and now we find ourselves in the grounds of **Northaw School**, part of the Norman Court estate, an independent school for children aged 3 to 14. The house dates back to the first half of the eighteenth century and was once owned by the Baring banking family. Norman Court was later acquired by Washington Singer of the famous Singer Sewing company. Make for the field corner and stile, cross the car park and skirt the hard tennis court. Waymarks enable us to navigate our way through the grounds with ease.

Pass the front of the school, keep to the right of some buildings and follow the path through the trees to reach the main drive. Turn

Mottisfont Abbey

left and walk away from Norman Court. When the drive bends left, take the waymarked path by the sign 'Home Stud Limited'. Pass between the buildings of the stud and head down to a kissing gate on the right. Follow the grassy path between the Old Rectory and the rooftops of **West Tytherley** and soon we reach some wooden steps taking us up to a viewing area overlooking a pretty lake. A seat allows us to enjoy a pleasant interlude.

Return to the main path and descend some steps into the village centre. The **Black Horse** is along to the left; our walk is to the right. Many of the village cottages we see here were once occupied by Norman Court estate workers. Pass the village primary school and then turn left at the sign for East Tytherley. West Tytherley's nineteenth-century church looms into view now and immediately beyond it we veer right, signposted **Frenchmoor**. Pass the Methodist church, which dates back to 1953, and keep right at the sign for Pug's Hole. Note the coppicing and the picturesque thatched cottages along this stretch of the road. Continue on the lane until we reach a right-hand bend. Turn left here into Bulls Drove and follow the track. By a thatched cottage we see a sign for Bentley Wood. The woodland owner allows public access and, if time allows, we can branch off at this point on a pleasant detour.

Returning to the walk, follow the sometimes waterlogged track through the woods, cross a lane leading to **Pug's Hole** and continue between the trees, keeping to the right of a thatched cottage. Avoid a stile leading into a field and look out for roe deer skipping gracefully through the woodland. Our route widens to a forest ride now and further on we pass another stile before skirting a field. Eventually we reach the road by a sign for **East Tytherley**. Go over to the car park of the **Star** inn and make for a gate on the far side. Cross the field to a gate in the next fence and then veer half right to a wrought-iron kissing gate in the woodland boundary. Follow the path to a stile and then cross a pasture towards woodland. Over to the left is Lockerley Hall, a Victorian Elizabethan-style mansion surrounded by pleasant parkland. Pass a small lake and cross a stream to a kissing gate. Go diagonally across the field towards woodland, making for a stile by two solitary trees set against the boundary.

Swing oblique left and aim for the curtain of woodland in the far distance. A stile and a galvanised gate gradually edge into view. Cross over to another stile in the field boundary and then follow the path through the woodland plantations. Keep left at a fork and go straight over at a track where there are 'no public rights of way' signs. Head for a junction and follow the sign for Mottisfont Abbey and village. Take the track and follow it to the road. Cross over to the double gates and then go diagonally across several pastures. Make for the field corner, exit to the road and turn left. At the junction we bear right for the centre of **Mottisfont**, back to where the walk began.

Walk 2 – The Silk Route

Whitchurch

Distance:	9½ miles
Start/Finish:	Whitchurch silk mill
Terrain:	Country lanes, farm tracks and field paths
Parking:	Free public car park in Winchester Street, adjoining the silk mill
Maps:	OS Landranger sheet 185 OS Explorer sheet 144
Refreshments:	Bourne Valley Inn and George Inn, St Mary Bourne. Silk mill tearooms and several pubs in Whitchurch town centre. Note: the pub at Binley, still marked on some maps, is now a private house.
Information:	Andover Tourist Information: 01264 324320 Whitchurch silk mill: 01256 892065

Now relieved of through traffic by the A34 and A303 trunk roads, Whitchurch is a thriving little country town on the banks of the fast flowing River Test. The river has spawned a number of mills along its length and, in Whitchurch, it has been turning the silk mill water wheel since the 1820s. The beautifully situated mill is now a working museum, producing high quality silks for theatrical costumes and interior furnishings. The mill has an attractive tea room and souvenir shop, and is open to the public six days a week.

Turn left out of the **car park** into Winchester Street and, at the five-way junction beyond the silk mill, turn left again into Bell Street. After 250 yards cross Lower Evingar Road and dive immediately through the old brick railway arch. Continue along the pavement on the right hand side, crossing three side roads – Hartley Meadow, Bloswood

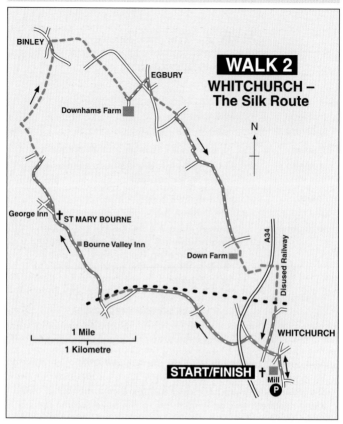

Drive and Meadow View. Fifty yards further on, cross the road and turn left where the wooden 'footpath' sign points our way up a farm track. The track curves to the right and passes under the A34 bridge, continuing through metal gates towards the trees on the brow of the hill. We pass a Dutch barn on our left and climb gently towards a line of electricity wires where the track levels out, carrying on between thick, well-trimmed hedges as far as the T junction at Cowdown Copse.

The track ends here, but our way lies straight ahead over the waymarked stile and into the woods. The path is narrow at first, but soon opens out into a woodland track, fringed in springtime by bluebells and primroses. A couple of hundred yards beyond the stile we fork right and drop gently down through young mixed planting, bearing to the left and drawing alongside a **railway cutting** on our right.

From here, we follow the railway for almost a mile. Our track drops below rail level and emerges onto an unclassified road by a brick railway arch on the right. Keep straight ahead along the road for 200 yards, until it bears away left at a rough lay-by, where a footpath sign points our way along a field-edge path at the foot of the embankment. On the far side of the field we dodge through a gap in the hedge and turn right onto the B3048.

Almost at once the railway soars over our heads on a nine-arch brick viaduct, and we pass the Vitacress depot on our left at the start of the tramp north towards **St Mary Bourne**. It's about a mile into the village and, whilst the road isn't especially busy, the lack of a pavement means keeping a sharp eye out for traffic. On the outskirts of the village, the **Bourne Valley Inn** offers a welcome refreshment stop.

Continuing into the village we pass St Peter's church on the right-hand side, shaded by the massive old yew trees in the churchyard. *St Peter's dates from about 1153, though of course the building has been much altered and extended. The font, which is carved from black Tournai marble, is one of only seven similar examples in this country; four of them are in Hampshire, and were possibly imported by the Bishop of Winchester, Henri de Blois (1129–1174).*

A hundred yards beyond the church we fork half-right at the **George Inn** and begin the climb up Spring Hill Lane. After 600 yards the lane levels out and bears right; keep right at the junction and carry on for a further 300 yards to the stile and wooden footpath sign in the hedge on the left.

Jump the stile and head across the field to a second stile at the corner of a small wood. Beyond the stile a track crosses our route and, following the yellow waymarks, we climb another stile into a field with the woodland on our left. Turn half-right, and follow the cross-field path through an indistinct gap in the far hedge. A length of metal fence serves as a gate here, and behind us is a yellow waymark for walkers coming the *other way!* Now keep to the left-hand field edge, following it as far as the top corner of the field, where yellow waymarks on a gatepost point left and right along a farm track.

Turn right, and follow the track for 300 yards before dodging right and left at the field end and diving into a narrow, tree-shaded footpath guarded by an old railway sleeper gatepost. It's better than it looks, and soon leads out onto a farm track for two-thirds of a mile of fast, easy walking to the footpath sign on the Binley road. We turn left, and drop down towards **Binley**.

After 300 yards we come to a road junction, and turn right at the footpath sign opposite the red phone box. Follow the easy, field-edge track as it winds uphill beside the hedge on the left. On the brow of the hill the track levels out, and the hedge drops away to the left. Keep half-left here, across a mown grassy field, towards an indistinct yellow waymark at a gap in the far hedge. Bear right, through the gap, and cross the next field. On the far side of the field the path meets the hedge, dives inside it, and turns right to continue in the thickness of the hedge.

Persevere! After about 200 yards we jump the stile across our path and continue straight ahead, now with a wooden post and rail fence on our right-hand side. Soon we're dropping downhill to a minor road, with a gravelled garage entrance on the right. Zigzag left and right across the road, climbing once again on a field edge track with conifers and a tall hedge to the left. It's half a mile of pleasant walking, up and over the brow through small belts of conifer and mixed woodland.

The track ends at a minor road, with a pair of brick and flint cottages on the left. We turn left here and follow the road for 400 yards, past **Egbury Farm**, to a T junction. Turn right, passing an enchanting group of thatched cottages, as far as the wooden bridleway sign 200 yards further on. Fork left onto the broad green bridleway, sticking with it as it zigzags right and left across the little road to Dunley. For the next 1½ miles this easy-to-follow farm track leads us south. The track kinks right and left on the line of Portway – the Roman road between Silchester and Old Sarum – and two hundred yards further on rises to a three-way bridleway signpost.

Keep left here; half a mile further on, waymarked footpaths cross our route, and we pass under some electricity power lines. After a further half mile we cross a minor road; follow the obvious right and left zigzag between the buildings at **Down Farm** and, beyond the farm, keep straight ahead along the edge of a field. The next 600 yards take us around two sides of this field, always with a hedge on our right for company. At the corner of the field we swing left, then briefly left again and back to the right, finally leaving the field by a metal-gated footbridge over the A34.

Beyond the bridge bear slightly left on a short cross-field path, studded by two conspicuous oak trees. A metal gate on the far side of the field leads onto an old railway bridge, but we turn right before the bridge, keeping the **disused railway** cutting on our left. The path drops steadily down to the level of the old railway, where a waymarked stile and metal farm gates lead us onto the old line. We stay on our southerly course, heading towards the massive brick arch under the London to Salisbury railway.

Whitchurch once lay at a 'crossroads' between the London & South Western Railway's London–Salisbury line, and the Great Western's Newbury–Winchester route. Yet passengers were denied a convenient interchange, for the rival companies built their stations a good half mile apart. During the Second World War the old Great Western line was upgraded to carry munitions and supplies for the 1944 Normandy landings. But memories are short, and the line we're now treading was closed during the early 1960s. Many miles of the old trackbed now lie buried under the A34 trunk road.

Almost at once, just opposite some old concrete lineside huts, fork off to the left and drop down to pass under the main line through a smaller brick arch. On the south side of the railway our path follows its own green tunnel; warehouses back onto the left-hand side of the path and, after 200 yards, we climb gently up to Evingar Road. **Whitchurch** railway station lies back up the road to our left, but we keep straight ahead, following Evingar Road seamlessly into Lower Evingar Road. After half a mile, at the bottom of the hill, we turn left into Bell Street and retrace our outward route to the **car park** in Winchester Street.

Walk 3 – Cobbett Country

Hurstbourne Tarrant

Distance:	8 miles
Start/Finish:	Hurstbourne Tarrant recreation ground
Terrain:	Field paths, tracks and several stretches of country road. Steep, sometimes slippery descent through Doles Wood, near the end of the walk
Parking:	Free car park at the start
Map:	OS Landranger sheet 185 OS Explorer sheet 131
Refreshments:	The George & Dragon, Hurstbourne Tarrant
Information:	Andover Tourist Information Centre: 01264 324320

Sheltering snugly in a gloriously verdant, steep-sided valley, Hurstbourne Tarrant is the quintessential English village, as well as the meeting point for two of Hampshire's smaller, lesser-known waterways – the Bourne rivulet and the River Swift. A long main street, groups of thatched cottages and a picturesque seventeenth-century coaching inn at the foot of a steep hill create an atmosphere of charm and quiet dignity. However, there is more to Hurstbourne Tarrant than a casual stroll through the village might reveal. The 'Tarrant' comes from the Dorset village of Tarrant Crawford, whose nuns owned land here, but it was William Cobbett who really put the place on the map, calling the village 'Uphusband' and writing about it in glowing, fulsome terms in his **Rural Rides.** *Cobbett travelled widely, but of all the places he visited, Hurstbourne Tarrant was his favourite village – 'a sight worth going many miles to see,' he claimed. He was equally flattering about the spectacular countryside which surrounds*

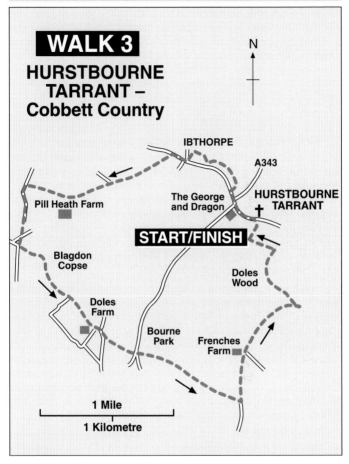

WALK 3

HURSTBOURNE TARRANT –
Cobbett Country

N

IBTHORPE

A343

Pill Heath Farm

The George
and Dragon

HURSTBOURNE
TARRANT

START/FINISH

Blagdon
Copse

Doles
Wood

Doles
Farm

Bourne
Park

Frenches
Farm

1 Mile

1 Kilometre

Hurstbourne Tarrant, forming the backdrop for this very pleasant circular walk. 'To stand upon any of the hills and look around you, you almost think you see the ups and downs of sea in a heavy swell... The undulations are endless, and the great variety in the... little hills has a very delightful effect.'

Leave the **car park**, just off the B3048 road to St Mary Bourne, and make for the flint church, a squat building with a weather-boarded bell turret topped by a spire. St Peter's has a medieval wall painting depicting the legend of the three living kings and the three dead kings. Sources suggest that three kings meet three skeletons while out hunting, reminding them of their own mortality. The main part of the church dates from the late twelfth and early thirteenth centuries.

Follow the road through the village to the A343. The striking façade of the **George & Dragon** catches our eye as we scan the road for traffic. It would be tempting to stop here for a drink, but far better to call in on our return when the physical effort of the walk is at last behind us. Turning right for a few steps brings us to the road for Ibthorpe and Upton. Follow the road towards the outer edge of Hurstbourne Tarrant and look for a kissing gate by the village hall. At this early stage of the walk we are following a stretch of the Test Way. Keep left along the field edge, the delightful little Swift trickling almost unseen beside us. Cross the next field and pass through three gates to arrive at a track. Turn left here and then veer right at the metalled lane, following it round to the left.

Make for a junction by a thatched cottage and, turning left, we soon reach the **Ibthorpe** to Upton road. *On the right here is Ibthorpe House, a fine Georgian building of chequered brick, where Jane Austen often stayed with her friends, the Lloyds. She is known to have attended church services at neighbouring Hurstbourne Tarrant.* Our route is to the right here, briefly along the road in a north-westerly direction. As the road begins to curve, take the stony drove road on the left. The track climbs steadily between the trees and after more than half a mile we reach a fork. Keep left here, then right at the next fork and keep going along the track. Eventually we reach the road.

Turn left and cross this remote, undiscovered north-west corner of Hampshire. Pass a small reservoir and pause at a gateway on the right to drink in a glorious view of distant countryside. We continue along the road, essentially quiet and free of traffic, passing a turning on the left for Hurstbourne Tarrant and Newbury. Note the old-style signpost here – black writing on a white background. During the Second World War these signs were constantly uprooted or moved, in order to confuse the enemy in the event of England being invaded.

Rowing boats at Colt Wharf, Odiham, on the Basingstoke Canal (Walk 5)

A fishing hut on the River Test, near Stockbridge (Walk 4)

The Basingstoke Canal, near Odiham (Walk 5)

Hurstbourne Tarrant

Follow the lane beyond **Pill Heath** House and turn left opposite a minor road on the right. We keep close to a line of trees, crossing into the next field via a stile located by some light woodland. Follow the field edge, keeping the protective curtain of trees close by us on the left.

Look for a redundant stile in the field corner and join a broad, enclosed track cutting between the wood and the field. Eventually we come to a cluster of remote, abandoned farm outbuildings – all that is left, in fact, of **Doles Farm**. Once, this place would have been a hive of activity as those who worked here busied themselves with the day to day business of running a farm. All that has gone and now the boarded-up brick and flint cottages and the ruinous buildings are silent.

The route of the walk requires careful negotiation at this point. Do not turn sharp right alongside the cottages; instead, keep left and follow the track as it curves to the right. Almost immediately, a footpath sign comes into view on the left. Avoid this and continue on the track as it sweeps to the right. Keep left at the fork and pass through a wide gate. Branch off half-left and follow the path through the trees, keeping close to the edge of the wood. There are teasing glimpses of open fields as we head for the main A343. Bear left at the road for a few yards before turning sharp right to join a rough track. The busy road is an unwelcome intrusion on our delightful walk but the ugly scar on the landscape is soon forgotten as we head back into the depths of the countryside.

No sooner do we join the track than we branch off it to cross the stile. Make for the field corner and pass through two gates to continue ahead in the next field. Glancing to the left we are treated to an impressive view of **Bourne Park**, a private house set in its own extensive grounds. Continue to maintain the same direction across country and further on we come to a sign for Rag Copse. Join a woodland track and here we pick our way between the trees, crossing another track after about 75 yards. Pass a sign for Long Copse and continue along the woodland edge, keeping fields on the left. We plunge ever further into the woods and eventually come down to a track by Frenches Lodge, a picturesque thatched cottage.

Turn left and follow the drive to **Frenches Farm**. Pass the farmhouse and then take the track round to the right between barns and brick outbuildings. Keep left and pass through three gates on our way towards distant woodland. Once through the third gate continue ahead across the field, keeping to the right of a reservoir. Swing right on approaching the trees and follow the field edge to a stile in the corner. Go straight over and keep ahead. Look for a hidden gate and stile and rejoin the Test Way by a sign for Wallop Hill Down. Follow the track through the woodland and in a while we reach a fork with a reassuring Test Way arrow. Keep right here to a stile and then follow the path down through the trees to the woodland edge.

Hurstbourne Tarrant lies ahead of us in the valley as we head down the field. Turn left at the bottom and follow the track along the field edge; the church and village buildings are clearly visible here. On reaching some barns, we turn right and make for the recreation ground **car park** where the walk began. For a well-earned drink at the George & Dragon, follow the road again to the centre of the village.

Walk 4 – Discovering Danebury Ring

Stockbridge

Distance:	9½ miles
Start/Finish:	Stockbridge
Terrain:	Downland paths and tracks, disused railway track, stretches of road
Parking:	Free parking in Stockbridge High Street (A30)
Map:	OS Landranger sheet 185 OS Explorer sheet 131
Refreshments:	Plenty to choose from in Stockbridge. The Mayfly at Testcombe. Space to picnic at Danebury Ring
Information:	Andover Tourist Information Centre: 01264 324320 Tourism Officer, Test Valley Borough Council: 01264 368836

Stockbridge is one of the world's most important fishing centres, with the impressive early nineteenth-century Grosvenor Hotel in the High Street playing host to those who hope that a few hours spent beside the tranquil waters of the Test may prove fruitful. The hotel is the headquarters of the prestigious Houghton Club and the walls of its clubroom are covered with glass cases containing enormous stuffed brown trout, the fish of the upper Test. Founded in 1822, the Houghton Club is restricted to less than 20 members. The Grosvenor's ample and distinctive overhanging porch, something of a landmark in Stockbridge, was built to prevent guests from getting wet as they arrived and departed in their carriages.

With its broad street of Tudor and Georgian houses, Stockbridge gives the impression of being a town of some size, though there is little

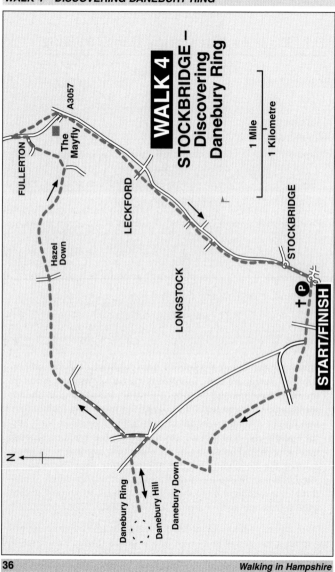

WALK 4
STOCKBRIDGE –
Discovering
Danebury Ring

1 Mile
1 Kilometre

A3057

FULLERTON

The Mayfly

LECKFORD

Hazel
Down

LONGSTOCK

STOCKBRIDGE

P

START/FINISH

N

Danebury Ring

Danebury Hill

Danebury Down

more to it than this main thoroughfare. Until the 1832 Reform Bill, Stockbridge was the most corrupt of all boroughs, stuck fast in the mire of political sleaze and electoral malpractice. It is said that when Sir Richard Steele of The Spectator *was seeking re-election in the town, he promised an apple stuffed with guineas to the first couple who could produce an off-spring nine months after he was elected. Steele didn't get in, so he wasn't obliged to fulfil his promise. Between 1562 and 1832 the 70 voters on the electoral roll returned two members to parliament. In the late seventeenth century a vote could be purchased for five guineas; by 1790 the rate was about 70 guineas and by 1831 it was one thousand pounds.*

Heading west along the A30, we pass **St Peter's** church and an assortment of antique shops, inns and tearooms. Crossing the Test we now we make a brief detour to look at an interesting, if somewhat curious, Welsh inscription which adorns the wall of a picturesque thatched cottage, known as the Drovers House, just a few yards along the road to Houghton. The name of the cottage is a clue, and, roughly translated, the inscription means 'seasoned hay, tasty pastures, good beer, comfortable beds'! It was here that sheep drovers broke their journey on their way from Wales to the Hampshire fairs.

Back on the A30, we begin a moderately steep ascent, trying to blot out the passing traffic as it thunders by. As the road bends right, take the turning signposted Test Valley School. Walk up the hill and when the road bends left, we continue ahead on a grassy track, formerly a Roman road. Vegetation lines our route and further on, when the bushes and undergrowth thin, we catch a breathtaking view of the Wiltshire Downs on the far horizon. Turn right at a stile, just before a track and some farm outbuildings, and return to the A30. Cross over to a stile and follow the field's right-hand boundary. **Danebury Hill** stands out clearly on the horizon at this stage of the route. Soon we are in the midst of an undulating, prairie-like landscape, with few obvious features and no hope of sheltering from any rain should dark clouds loom over the horizon.

Crops are sown almost to the edge of the fields, so expect to find the boundary paths very narrow in places. As we sweep left in the field corner, note how grazing pigs have steadily eroded any vegetation here. Join a broad grassy track to a gate and stile. Turn right and follow the downland track. If we look over to the left at this point, we may just pick out the remains of the old Stockbridge Racecourse stadium, almost completely enveloped by trees.

There was a racecourse here until 1898, playing host to many important meetings in the racing world. Many top horses and riders raced at Stockbridge, and crowds from far and wide came to witness the colourful spectacle. Then, at the end of the last century, race meetings switched to Salisbury where there is still a racecourse today. The old ruined stadium serves as an eerie monument to the days when this open downland was alive with the sound of cheering crowds and the thud of galloping hooves, and men and women strolled around the place in their Victorian dress, placing their bets and savouring the thrill of the race.

Take the track up the slope to the road junction. Here we have a choice. To visit **Danebury Ring**, turn left and follow the road for about a quarter of a mile to the main entrance. *Danebury Ring was once an important Iron Age hill fort which covered an oval area of 13 acres in the form of cleverly constructed ditches and ramparts. There have been excavations in progress at Danebury since 1969 and a great deal of the site's history has been pieced together as a result of the work. Although much of this evidence remains inconclusive, what is known is that the last significant re-building at the start of the 1st century BC was never finished. Around 500 people lived here in wattle houses, ploughing the land, eating coarse bread, drinking beer and bartering with neighbouring tribes. All the time, they feared invasion or attack; they chose this hilltop site because it enabled them to see over many miles. Today, Danebury is a popular amenity area, run by Hampshire County Council, but the eerie sense of ancient history still pervades these downland slopes.*

To continue the main walk, go straight over and take the first track, a byway, on the right, by a row of fir trees. Pass a brick and flint building on the left and stride out between fields and downland slopes. Go straight on when the track curves right, passing beneath a height restricting bar. Our route now is over a narrower, grassier track with the surroundings consisting of scrub and semi-wooded downland. Cross over at the next road and keep right when the track forks, cutting between fields. Turn left at the next road and stay on the right to face the oncoming traffic. Pass lines of cottages at **Fullerton**, so small it is barely a hamlet, and keep right at the next junction. A few steps along the road brings us to a delightful spot on the River Anton. Glancing to the right reveals a charming old mill nestling among trees and meadows. Less than a mile downstream from here the river meets the Test.

Turn left at the T junction and head briefly along the A3057 towards Andover. Cross the bridge and turn sharp right by the post box and the 'slow' sign painted on the road. Now we begin a long stretch of a disused railway track. *The line, designed to link London and Salisbury with Andover and Southampton, was greatly appreciated by Queen Victoria who used this route when travelling to Osborne House, her holiday home on the Isle of Wight.* Pass the old station house on the right and further on we come to the remains of Fullerton station.

Rejoining the Test Way we follow the trail through a tunnel of trees and across the meandering Test. The sturdy sleepers on the bridge recall the golden age of railway travel when the leviathans of steam roared along this line. Keep on the track bed as far as the next bridge, where we have a choice of routes. On a warm day, particularly at the height of summer, it makes sense to break our journey at this point and head in the direction of the **Mayfly**, one of Hampshire's loveliest riverside inns. To do so, turn left immediately before the bridge and follow the path alongside the brick wall. Bear right at the road and right again at the junction.

Suitably refreshed, return to the Test Way and follow the track bed, passing under the bridge. The shaded path courts the river on the approach to Longstock and Stockbridge. This closing stage of the walk is a delight at any time of the year, but particularly on a fine day with the sun dancing between the trees and the sparkling river snaking through the countryside. As the sound of traffic begins to fade and the track moves away from the road, we come to a giant sycamore tree on the left. Pass two bridges at the village of **Leckford** and on this stretch we can hear the soothing sound of water through the trees.

Pass under the next road bridge and look for a path on the right, swinging back and up to the road. Turn left and walk along to the

Test. *The water is so clear because it comes from rainfall that is filtered by natural processes – cleansed by underground chalk springs. Little thatched fishing huts, used for storing tackle, can be seen up and down river, and along the bridges are eel traps, now purely decorative and made of iron. There was once a Danish Dock in the adjoining water meadows, created for the Dane's flat-bottomed boats and built in the form of a wide waterway extending to about 300 feet. The dock may well have been used as a base camp for further exploration and development and as a kind of depot through which supplies and materials could be despatched to settlers.*

Return to the Test Way and follow it south towards **Stockbridge**. Join the A3057 and keep to the verge, veering right at the roundabout, then right again at the next junction for Stockbridge High Street. Afternoon tea at The Grosvenor seems a civilised way to round off one of Hampshire's most spectacular downland walks.

Walk 5 – By the Basingstoke Canal

Odiham

Distance:	7 miles
Start/Finish:	Odiham
Terrain:	Field and woodland paths, canal towpath, brief stretches of road
Parking:	Parking available in the High Street
Map:	OS Landranger sheet 186 OS Explorer sheet 144
Refreshments:	Plenty to choose from in Odiham. Several pubs in North Warnborough; The Fox and Goose at Greywell
Information:	Farnham Tourist Information Centre: 01252 715109

No visit to this corner of Hampshire is complete without a visit to Odiham, considered by many to be a jewel among the smaller towns of southern England. Handsome buildings line its High Street, and a liberal sprinkling of Odiham's houses are Tudor and Georgian; some are timber-framed, which was common before local bricks came into general use in the eighteenth century. The Priory and neighbouring Palace Gate Farm were once part of a Tudor Palace visited by Queen Elizabeth I. French soldiers were held as prisoners at Odiham during the Napoleonic wars, living in a camp dug out of an old chalk pit on the Alton road. According to some sources, they also helped construct the nearby Basingstoke Canal. Odiham churchyard contains the graves of several prisoners.

All Saints is the largest church in North Hampshire and includes a seventeenth-century gallery staircase, a thirteenth-century chalk font and an impressive pulpit carved with scrolls and vases of flowers. Near the church is a 'Pest House' into which were incarcerated suspected plague sufferers.

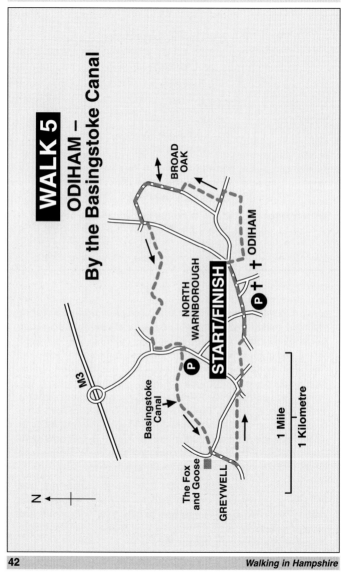

WALK 5

ODIHAM –
By the Basingstoke Canal

BROAD OAK

ODIHAM

NORTH WARNBOROUGH

START/FINISH

M3

Basingstoke Canal

The Fox and Goose

GREYWELL

1 Mile

1 Kilometre

N

From the centre of **Odiham** our route is east along the High Street. We pass a turning on the left to the Basingstoke Canal and then turn right just beyond it to join a footpath. Go through a gate, cross a road and continue between houses through the outskirts of Odiham. It is largely residential here and the thought of field paths and quiet woodland ahead seems a pleasing prospect. Soon we cross another road and follow a path between wooden panel fencing. Before very long we come to a stile on the extreme southern edge of the town. We have reached the countryside at last! Turn left and follow the field boundary; cross a stile, pass a wrought-iron kissing gate on the left and make for a stretch of raised path. Cross two stiles into a field on the left and head diagonally right to the right edge of a hedgerow. The path is waymarked here. Follow the path, with the hedgerow on the left, cross a footbridge and make for a stile in the field corner.

At this point we turn left along a disused road to reach the A287. Cross over to a footpath at Penarth Stud, keeping to the left of the buildings. Now we follow the path over several stiles, along the edge of a paddock and through the trees to the corner of a large field. Keep close to the left edge until a thatched cottage is reached on the left. Turn left just beyond it to cross a footbridge, then follow the path onto a drive and bear right at the T junction, opposite Wincombe Cottage.

Follow the lane, crossing over the Basingstoke Canal at **Broad Oak Bridge**. *Completed in 1794, the Basingstoke Canal was originally planned to link London and Guildford with Southampton. Vessels plied the waterway carrying grain, coal, malt and farm produce. However, the canal's fortunes were never particularly good and eventually the western end was filled in. It later reopened following major restoration work.*

Making a brief but worthwhile detour at this stage of the walk, we turn right to follow the towpath for several hundred yards until we come to a path which is not actually a public right of way. However, this stretch of the canal does offer tantalizing glimpses of King John's Hunting Lodge which occupies a magical, secluded setting amid the trees. *The lodge, noted for its exuberant gables, dates back to the mid-eighteenth century and was built as an eyecatcher for the occupants of Dogmersfield Park, a nearby estate. However, the profusion of trees now obscures the view. The style of the house is Jacobean but the association with King John is not known.*

Return to Broad Oak Bridge, turn right for several steps to a common bylaws sign and take the middle of three paths through the woodland. On reaching a drive, we turn left and make for the road. Bear left here and follow Bagwell Lane to the junction with London Road. Turn left and then almost immediately right at the next footpath sign. Aim for a stile, cross a paddock to a double stile and then go slightly left in the next field to another stile. Cross the next field to a barred gate and continue to a double stile in the far boundary. Cross a farm track to a stile and then walk diagonally across a large field, aiming for the arch of the bridge over the bypass. Reach the corner and go forwards across the turf for about 50 yards to a stile.

Head obliquely up the bank to another stile and bear left over the bridge. Walk down to the **Basingstoke Canal**. Bear right and follow the waterway, passing an entrance to the garden of the Jolly Miller at **North Warnborough**. Go under the road bridge and further on we reach a swing road bridge by some cottages. Press on along the towpath and soon we arrive at the entrance to King John's Castle on the right.

The castle was used by King John as a place to rest and hunt on his journeys from Windsor to Winchester. It was from here, one summer's day in 1215, that he set off to sign the Magna Carta at Runnymede. The following year the castle managed to hold out for two weeks against an attack by a French expeditionary force under the Dauphin. King David of Scotland was held captive in the castle for ten long years in the fourteenth century. Today, only the octagonal keep survives but, in a certain light in the depths of winter, the castle ruin is wonderfully eerie, the lengthening shadows, the crumbling walls and the setting sun creating a really spooky atmosphere. We almost expect to see the figure of King John in our midst.

Leaving the ruined stronghold, we continue along the towpath, passing over the River Whitewater and beside the remains of a disused lock. Ahead of us now is the outline of Greywell Tunnel, built about 1792 and intended as a short cut to save the Basingstoke Canal a winding 6-mile trip across country. *The tunnel, at an overall distance of 1230 yards (nearly a mile), became one of the longest in* the south of England. It collapsed in 1872 immediately after a very fortunate bargee had passed through it. The damage was repaired but it collapsed again, 60 years later, in 1932. Like many other canal tunnels, it had no towpath and so bargees were forced to 'leg it' – a slow and laborious process which involved using their legs against the walls of the cold dark passage in order to manoeuvre themselves through it. Today, the tunnel has huge ecological importance as it is the largest known bat roost in Britain. Up to 12,500 bats of all native species hibernate here, and the tunnel has been declared a Site of Special Scientific Interest.

Take the path over its portal and drop down to the road. Turn right, then left at the junction, and walk through the village of **Greywell**. Continue along the road to the lychgate of St Mary's church, pass through a kissing gate and head diagonally across the field. Three-quarters of the way across it, swing right to join a woodland path, crossing the Whitewater to Greywell Moors Nature Reserve. Chalk springs rise here and flow through the marshy peat, on their way to join the river. This encourages orchids and marsh marigolds to thrive. Continue through the trees and pass the memorial to eminent botanist Ted Wallace. Go straight ahead to a stile and then veer obliquely left across a large field to a stile at the road.

Turn left for a few yards to a footpath on the right. Take the path, bearing left after several yards to cross a stile. Head diagonally across a paddock, cross another stile and maintain the same direction, heading obliquely across the field to the next stile. Cross the road to the stile opposite; in the field veer half-right towards a hedgerow. Aim for a stile located about 75 yards from its right-hand corner and cross over to join a path by a school. Turn right to the road and bear left. Our route is once more through the residential streets of **Odiham** as we begin the home straight. When the road veers left, go ahead into West Street and on to the main junction. Go straight over and back into Odiham.

Walk 6 – A Walk on Watership Down

Kingsclere

Distance:	10 miles
Start/Finish:	St Mary's Church, Kingsclere
Terrain:	Field paths and downland tracks; several climbs
Parking:	Car park off Anchor Road, Kingsclere, opposite the church
Map:	OS Landranger sheet 174 OS Explorer sheet 144
Refreshments:	Several pubs in Kingsclere; The Vine, Hannington
Information:	Basingstoke Tourist Information Centre: 01256 817618 Newbury Tourist Information Centre: 01635 30267

The village of Kingsclere can be traced back to Saxon times, though there were people living here before then. The West Saxons hated city life and the downland area in which the village lies would have been an ideal spot for a settlement with a constant supply of water always available and plentiful pasture for the animals. The woodland, too, would have yielded fuel and timber for building. The name Kingsclere was spelt Klere in the ninth century, Cleare or Clera in the tenth century, and Clere in the eleventh. By the thirteenth century, as a result of visits by various Kings to nearby Freemantle, where King Henry II built a royal hunting lodge, it had become known as Kyngescler. During the Civil War, King Charles I spent the night of 21 October 1644 at Frobury Manor House, about a mile to the north-west of the village.

Famous for its horse-racing connections, Kingsclere has boasted some fine winners in its time. At the end of the nineteenth century John Porter's stables produced six Derby winners and more recently the village was the home of Mill Reef.

We begin at the Norman church of **St Mary's**, heavily restored in 1848-49, though the north doorway is original. *The church was once paved with medieval floor tiles and later the walls of the chapel were hung with them. St Mary's contains magnificent monuments to Sir Henry Kingsmill and his wife, Lady Bridget.* Once in the churchyard take the tarmac path on the far side. Pass a pond on the right and turn right by a wooden panel fence. Cross several bridges and turn left. Soon we bear right to follow a path between fences to a wrought-iron kissing gate leading out to the road. Turn left and head out of Kingsclere; ahead of us now are memorable views up towards Watership Down.

Continue to a white gate and opening on the left. Skirt the field along a broad grassy path until we come to a gap in the boundary. Follow the path between fields, heading towards the slopes of Watership Down and Cannon Heath Down. On reaching a junction with a clear track, turn right and head west. Make for a line of trees at right-angles to the track and turn left to join a path running up through a tongue of woodland to a stile. Climbing steeply now, we aim diagonally right across the slopes of the escarpment, keeping the fence on the left. Make for a stile and go slightly left. Cross the all-weather gallops and go diagonally across the grass towards some bushes. Now, we find ourselves on the edge of **Watership Down**.

This breezy downland is the very private domain of those now legendary rabbits in the classic tale of the same name by local author Richard Adams. With its legendary associations, the reality of a visit to this lonely scarp does little to destroy the rare, magical quality of the book. Fortunately, the place has never been commercialised, so it remains quiet and undiscovered – just as it is in the story.

If we are feeling particularly energetic, we can extend the walk at this point by following the track west over the grassy down to a line of sturdy old beeches by the road. *With the breeze sighing gently in the branches above us, we can look down to Sydmonton Court, a large country house set in its own beautiful and extensive parkland*

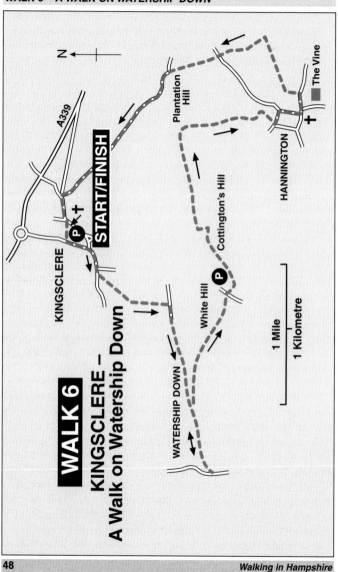

WALK 6
KINGSCLERE –
A Walk on Watership Down

and now the home of composer Sir Andrew Lloyd Webber. However, with much of the walk still in front of us, we mustn't allow ourselves to dwell here for too long – glorious though the views are. Head back along the chalk track, part of the Wayfarer's Walk, following it all the way to the B3051 road at **White Hill**. Along the way we cross the top of Cannon Heath Down.

The name comes from the link with the Canons of Rouen in France. Henry I granted the Manor of Kingsclere to the Canons of the Church of St Mary at Rouen. They held it almost uninterrupted until 1335 and its revenue helped to build Rouen Cathedral.

Cross the road and bear right by the entrance to the **car park**, still following the Wayfarer's Walk. Cut between trees and undergrowth, making for a stile and gate on the left. Cross over and skirt the field edge, keeping the fence on the right. Aim for the Hannington television mast and approach a double stile in the field corner. Cross over, keep the field boundary on the right and make for a galvanised gate and stile. Don't cross it; instead, we go left and follow the perimeter fence to its corner. Continue down the field to a stile and footpath sign. Turn right and follow the path along the woodland edge. Eventually we cross an open field to reach a bridle track. Bear right and go straight on at a junction of tracks. Cross the line of the Portway, seen clearly on the map but not visible on the ground.

The Romans began building roads soon after the invasion of AD43, and the network eventually covered all of Roman Britain. To begin with, the roads were designed to meet military needs, but in time they became vital trade and communications routes, helping and improving the local economy. The Portway, a typical Roman road, ran from Calleva, better known today as Silchester, on the Hampshire/Berkshire border near Reading, to Old Sarum in Wiltshire.

Follow the track to the left, then the right, and make for a gate in the field corner. Turn left and follow the road to the junction, bearing right for **Hannington**. On reaching the spacious village green we have a choice. On a warm day we might be thinking in terms of a drink at this stage of the walk. If so, continue for a short distance to the **Vine**. To continue the walk take the turning opposite the green and church and follow it to Bertha's Cottage, bearing left by Michael's Field.

Now follow the track to a bridleway sign and bear right. Take the

The Crown pub at Kingsclere

clear track across the fields to the next junction, turn left and follow the bridleway down to a road. Cross over and continue on the bridle track, recrossing the Portway once more. Climb to a junction, veer right towards **Plantation Hill** and follow the track towards houses and farm buildings. Keep ahead on a tarmac road, with a white fence on the right. When it curves right we go straight on down a very pleasant green lane, which provides impressive views up towards White Hill and the television mast. Pass a bridleway running off sharp left and keep right at the fork just beyond. Join a tarmac path cutting between houses on the edge of **Kingsclere** and follow it down to the main road. Bear left and walk down George Street into the centre of the village. Have a leisurely look at Kingsclere and its striking buildings before returning to the car park.

Walk 7 – The Portals' Paper Chase

Whitchurch and Overton

Distance:	**5 miles**
Start:	**Overton railway station**
Finish:	**Whitchurch railway station**
Terrain:	**Mainly byways and quiet roads**
Parking:	**Small car parks at both Overton and Whitchurch stations**
Maps:	**OS Landranger sheet 185**
	OS Explorer sheet 144
Refreshments:	**Watership Down Inn, Freefolk**
Information:	**Andover Tourist Information: 01264 324320**

In 1712 a Huguenot refugee by the name of Henri de Portal set up a paper-making business at Bere Mill in Whitchurch. The firm moved east to the newly completed Laverstoke Mill in 1719, and five years later de Portal won the contract to supply paper for Bank of England notes. In later years the company moved east once again, and Portals was recently acquired by the De La Rue group.

The firm still produces banknote paper here – but could this quiet corner of Hampshire have given us more than just the folding stuff in our wallets? Although my dictionary lists 'quid' as slang for a pound, it notes that the word's origin is obscure. Perhaps it is; but I can't help wondering if – like banknote paper itself – the expression comes from Overton Mill in Quidhampton ...

Leave **Overton station** by the private footpath beside the footbridge steps on the northern platform. (This path belongs to Portals, but is normally open for public use). Turn left at the end of the path, and follow the green track that runs between the factory gate and Portals car park, keeping the high chain link fence to the left. We climb

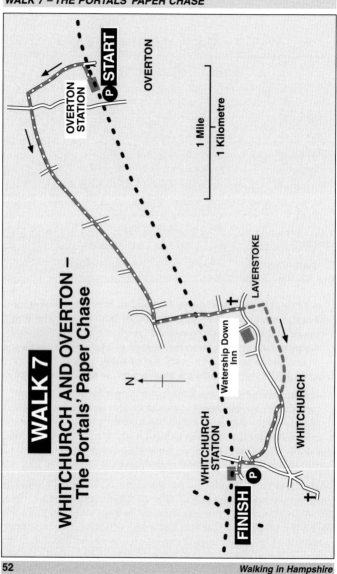

gently for the first couple of hundred yards with the factory boundary on the left; then we leave it behind, and follow this pleasant rural lane with hedges on both sides. Half a mile further on we come to a T junction, and turn left at the three-way byway signpost.

Now we're heading west through a charming tunnel of low hawthorn trees and, after a couple of hundred yards, we zigzag right and left across the B3051 road. The first 100 yards beyond the road have been eroded by motorbikes, but the track soon settles into its stride and presses onwards through a varied mixture of light woodland. Follow it for a couple of miles, as far as the first metalled road since leaving the B3051.

This is Watch Lane; turn left, and follow this sleepy little road as it climbs gently between thick hedges, then drops lazily over the brow to cross the railway at Southview Cottages. Pass the turning to Overton Rugby Club on the left, and a row of brick cottages on the right, and keep straight ahead as the lane dives through a wooded chalk cutting to reach the B3400 at Freefolk.

Just to the left, look out for the charming crescent of thatched cottages facing the main road. With their half-timbered gables and pretty communal gardens, Manor Cottages evoke an altogether less hurried, more tranquil way of life. *Yet, ironically, these lovely Arts and Crafts style houses were built by Lord Portal of Laverstoke in 1939 – at the outbreak of the Second World War. Just across the road a large wooden cross stands above a semi-circular stone seat. Around the worn stonework runs the barely legible inscription 'Rest here awhile beneath the sign of love which tells thee of eternal rest above'.*

By all means take a break here, or we can make the short diversion to the **Watership Down Inn**. To get to the pub, turn right at the bottom of Watch Lane, and follow the main road towards **Whitchurch** for 200 yards. Then turn right again up Priory Lane to the pub on the left-hand side.

To continue our walk from the bottom of Watch Lane, cross the main road and keep straight on at the wooden footpath sign; then, almost at once, bear left over a small wooden footbridge. Follow the path as it winds briefly through a small meadow to a larger wooden bridge over the River Test. On the far side of the bridge follow the waymark to the left, and cross the metal sluice gates to the waymarked wicket gate. Then keep straight ahead to the waymarked stile at the top left corner of a small paddock; jump over and carry straight on, keeping the small group of trees on the right and the brick and flint cottages on the left.

At the far side of the field we turn right and follow the boundary fence on our left, passing into the next field by a large, stag-headed oak tree. Still with the wire fence for company, we come to an iron bench and a stile beneath the line of trees on the far side of the field. Nip over the stile, and follow the waymarked route towards the red-brick cottage across the next field. Climb the step-stile just to the left of the cottage, then keep straight on for 50 yards and cross a further stile beside the five-bar gate.

Here we join a metalled drive, cross an ornamental brick bridge, and continue for a quarter of a mile to emerge once again onto the B3400. Turn left here, and follow the main road for 100 yards before forking right into Lynch Hill Park. The road climbs steadily through an area of attractive housing, and we follow it all the way to the top of the hill where it bears left and briefly joins Dances Lane before emerging onto Newbury Street. This is the old Whitchurch to Newbury road; turn right for 200 yards, then left into Station Road to finish at **Whitchurch station**.

Walk 8 – Hiking to Hannington

Overton and Hannington

Distance:	**9½ miles**
Start/Finish:	**Overton railway station**
Terrain:	**Mainly byways and quiet roads**
Parking:	**Small car park at Overton station**
Maps:	**OS Landranger sheet 185**
	OS Explorer sheet 144
Refreshments:	**The Vine Inn, Hannington**
Information:	**Andover Tourist Information: 01264 324320**

At the time of Domesday, Overton lay clustered around St Mary's church on the north side of the River Test. In AD909 King Edward had granted the land to Frithstan, Bishop of Winchester, and the town was destined to become the centre of a great episcopal manor. So it was that early in the thirteenth century, Bishop Godfrey de Lucy planned an entirely new town on the south bank of the river. The town's market was granted in 1218 by King Henry III, and by 1295 Overton was represented in Parliament by two of its burgesses – an expensive luxury that was scrapped after little more than a decade.

The original medieval village north of the river had virtually disappeared by the seventeenth century, and the town has been grappling with more modern problems for almost a hundred years. In 1909, Lord Portal noted that 'motors are racing through the village at well over 20mph, they must not exceed 10mph.' The job of enforcing the law was entrusted to constables armed with stop-watches and flags – a task now delegated to electronic speed cameras!

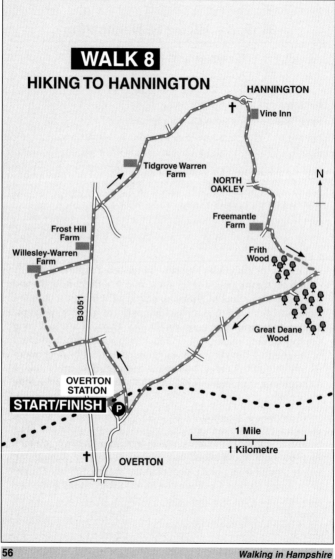

WALK 8
HIKING TO HANNINGTON

HANNINGTON

Vine Inn

Tidgrove Warren Farm

NORTH OAKLEY

Frost Hill Farm

Freemantle Farm

Willesley-Warren Farm

Frith Wood

B3051

Great Deane Wood

N

OVERTON STATION

START/FINISH

P

OVERTON

1 Mile

1 Kilometre

The first mile of this route follows the outward track of Walk 7, leaving **Overton station** by the footpath near the footbridge steps on the northern platform. Although this path belongs to the adjacent Portals paper mill, it is normally open for public use. Turn left at the end of the path and take the green track running between the factory gate and Portals car park. After a couple of hundred yards of gentle climb we leave the factory behind and continue northwards for half a mile to the T junction, where we turn left.

Continue westwards for 200 yards through a tunnel of over-hanging hawthorn trees, and zigzag right and left across the **B3051** road. There has been some erosion here from motorbikes, but the track soon settles down. We follow it for about 600 yards, dropping gently downhill to a small 'crossroads' marked by a wooden footpath sign. Here we turn right, and climb up through the gap in the hedge to the edge of an open field.

Keep left, and follow the hedgerow trees along the edge of the field for just over half a mile. At the north-west corner of the field we turn right onto a metalled farm road, and follow it past some attractive brick and flint cottages to rejoin the B3051 near the brick-built April Cottage. Turn left here, keeping a sharp eye out for traffic, and follow the main road over **Frost Hill**.

At the foot of the hill a metal public footpath sign points our way to the right, down a roughly surfaced lane. After 200 yards we cross a metalled by-road and continue along a tree-shaded gravelled road for the half mile to **Tidgrove Warren Farm**, where the track continues as a green lane. We climb gently but steadily for 400 yards before rounding a right-hand bend and cruising lazily over the summit.

Now the lane drops down to a metal farm gate. Pass around the side, cross the Wayfarer's Walk, and follow the yellow waymark pointing slightly leftwards across the open field ahead. This is skylark country; a wide landscape, with some fine views behind us. Pass into the next field at a wooden footpath sign, bear slightly to the right, and keep alongside the hedgerow on the right.

We approach **Hannington** on a delightful green footpath, with hedges now on both sides. The path climbs gently to a modern barn, and we keep straight ahead through the small wooden gate marked 'footpath only'. With a post and wire fence on our left we work our way around the back of a huge old timber barn, emerging on the village green by All Saints church.

Hannington lies high on the Hampshire downs, some 660 feet above sea level and at least 30 miles from the coast. So it seems ironic that the village's first appearance in recorded history links it with King Canute, better known for his exploits by the sea. Canute invaded England in 1015 and took the English throne after the death of Ethelred's son, Edmund Ironside, in the following year. One of Canute's followers, Leofwine, had bought a substantial estate at Hannington from King Ethelred and, in 1023, Canute issued a charter confirming his ownership. The document included an Anglo-Saxon survey of the Hannington estate, and All Saints church also dates from this period. It is a charming little building of cut flints with a shingled bell-tower, and the south wall contains a stunningly beautiful engraved glass window dedicated to the farmer William Whistler.

Cross the green to the village road and turn right for the short stretch to the **Vine Inn**, where a notice by the door shows that we're expected: 'We welcome those who have been in the countryside' it says, 'but please don't bring the countryside in on your boots.'

Beyond the pub we follow the road for half a mile, dropping steadily downhill and rounding several bends to a road junction. *There's a letter box here, which recently carried an official notice that must surely be unique: 'Due to snail infestation,' it read, 'you are advised not to post mail in this box as the snails will eat your letters. Royal Mail apologises for any inconvenience this may cause you'.*

Turn left opposite the letter box, and follow the winding road for about 400 yards. Then, at a sharp left-hand bend, look out for the wooden footpath sign in the right-hand verge. A few yards further on, climb the right-hand bank and follow the field edge towards the left-hand corner of **Freemantle Farm**. Pass the duck pond, walk through the farmyard to the two-way footpath sign, and continue onto the Wayfarer's Walk straight ahead.

The gravelled farm road climbs gently to the crest of the hill. Follow it as it thrashes left and right under a line of electricity wires, then drop down the hill and swing left into **Frith Wood**. On the far side of the wood we meet the electricity wires once again. A Wayfarer's Walk waymark on one of the poles confirms our route, which briefly crosses an open area between two fields before plunging into the fringe of **Great Deane Wood**.

After 200 yards we come to an easily-overlooked waymark at a junction of the forest paths; turn left here for a short, overgrown section that ends at a gate and a stile. Nip over the stile and turn right, leaving the Wayfarer's Walk, and joining a delightful tree-shaded country lane. Three-quarters of a mile further on the lane emerges into an open, well-farmed landscape with views towards Ashe Warren House on our left. Now the end is in sight, and the tall chimneys of Portals paper mill beckon us on towards Overton station.

Soon we come to the road junction at Ashe Warren. Keep straight on here – and at the crossroads at Nutley Bottom – following the quiet byroads towards Overton. A mile further on the railway draws in from the left, and the road zigzags across it on a brick arched bridge. Four hundred yards beyond the railway we turn right at the T junction towards Overton Mill; soon we're diving under the railway and rejoining our outward route, back down the private path to **Overton station**.

Walk 9 – Hampshire Heartlands

The Candover Valley

Distance:	**10 miles**
Start/Finish:	**St Peter's church, Brown Candover**
Terrain:	**Byways and bridleways; will be muddy after rain**
Parking:	**Informal village parking: please take care not to cause obstruction or inconvenience**
Maps:	**OS Landranger sheet 185**
	OS Explorer sheet 132 and 144
Refreshments:	**The Queen Inn, Dummer**
Information:	**Basingstoke Tourist Information: 01256 817618**

The Candover valley remains one of Hampshire's hidden treasures; a timeless, well-wooded landscape of tiny villages and tightly folded hillsides. The area had the good fortune to be shunned by the M3; yet, up to now, the motorway has been an unexpectedly good neighbour, providing a barrier against Basingstoke's expansionist tendencies in the north. This charming, isolated route follows the well-maintained Wayfarer's Walk as far as Dummer, returning to Brown Candover over rural byways and the Oxdrove Way.

St Peter's church lies a hundred yards back from the B3046 Alresford to Basingstoke road, and forms a focus for the straggling village of Brown Candover. Leave the road at the **Wayfarer's Walk** waymark, and follow the left-hand edge of the playing fields to the corner of the churchyard. Here, a waymarked path leads over a stile and onto an attractive, sunken track that climbs gently uphill and away from the village.

Passing Church Lane Farm we continue along the waymarked

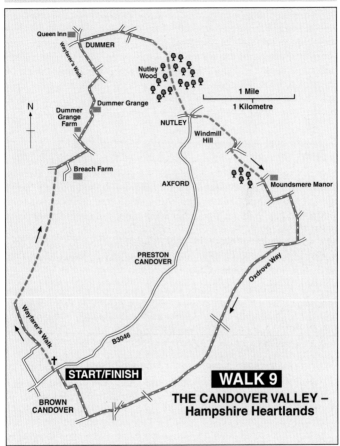

Queen Inn

Wayfarer's Walk

DUMMER

Nutley
Wood

1 Mile

1 Kilometre

N

Dummer Grange

Dummer
Grange
Farm

NUTLEY

Windmill
Hill

Breach Farm

AXFORD

Moundsmere Manor

PRESTON
CANDOVER

Wayfarer's Walk

Oxdrove Way

B3046

START/FINISH

WALK 9

BROWN
CANDOVER

THE CANDOVER VALLEY –
Hampshire Heartlands

route, an undulating path that offers brisk, easy walking with glimpses
of a well-farmed landscape beyond the tall hedgerows on either side.
At the end of the first mile we come to a five-bar gate where the
Wayfarer's Walk takes us through the gardens of Lone Barn. Beyond
the buildings we bear right, continuing along a hedged trackway for
the next half mile.

Now the hedges drop away, and we emerge onto the unfenced green track that crosses Beckett's Down in company with a line of newly planted saplings. Carry on past a small clump of beech trees near the summit of the Down, followed by an old chalk pit on the left-hand side. Here the waymarked path is once again shaded by hedgerow trees, and soon begins to drop downhill. A three-way 'right of way' sign at Lower Down Copse points us to the right, following the Wayfarer's Walk along a gravelled farm track.

The track upgrades to a metalled lane as we pass the imposing entrance to **Breach House** on the right-hand side. Swing left at the foot of the lane, past a pair of whitewashed cottages on the left-hand side. Two hundred yards further on we pass Summerfield Cottage before turning right at the wooden 'bridleway' sign that points up the drive to **Dummer Grange**. Our route side-steps the Grange at the second cattle grid, swinging hard left onto a gravelled track for a short, sharp climb. Now the track swings back to the right, and levels out for a couple of hundred yards; turn left at the T junction, and follow the waymarked route as it zigzags right and then left for the final mile into **Dummer** village.

Our track meets the village road at a second T junction; this time we turn right, and almost at once the Wayfarer's Walk swings back to the left, opposite All Saints church. Our own way lies straight ahead – though a short diversion to the left leads to a welcome refreshment break at the Queen Inn!

Back at the church, we take the lane signposted towards Farleigh and Ellisfield. It runs straight as an arrow for half a mile; then, 200 yards beyond the right-hand bend, the Farleigh Wallop road bears away to the left. Keep straight on here, and join the gravel track waymarked 'off-road cycle track'. We pass some cottages on the left, and after 400 yards the track swings off to the right; we slip away to the left, still following the 'off-road cycle track' waymarks.

Now the path drops downhill and bears right through **Nutley Wood** on a muddy, sunken way. We leave the woods near a chalk pit on the left hand side and emerge into a long thin clearing. Follow the path as it clings to the edge of the woods on our right, and keep straight on as it joins a gravelled track that drops gently down to Nutley Manor Farm.

Bear left through the farmyard, zigzag left and right across the village road, and rejoin the bridleway as it climbs the flank of **Windmill Hill**. Keep the field boundary on the left, and follow it over the brow of the hill and into a second field. Towards the bottom corner of this field, dodge through the small wooden wicket beside a field gate in the hedge on the left-hand side. Here, a green track drops down behind a small thatched cottage and leads us out onto the Axford byroad. Turn right for 50 yards, then left, where a wooden bridleway sign points our way up the hawthorn shaded track towards Moundsmere Manor.

More than 450 years ago, these lands formed part of the dower of Anne of Cleves, fourth wife of Henry VIII. Anne was Henry's blind date; her father John, Duke of Cleves, was a strong supporter of the Protestant faith in western Germany, and this fact seems to have outweighed all others in the arrangements that were made for her marriage to the King. By the time that Henry first set eyes upon his future Queen, the treaty for their betrothal was already signed. His disappointment at their meeting was complete; Anne could not speak English, neither did she share the King's great passion for music: 'If it were not to satisfy the world and my realm,' he told Cromwell before the wedding, 'I would not do that which I must do this day for none earthly thing.' The marriage was to last just six short months. Ill-starred from the beginning, the union was never consummated. Moreover, the political climate was changing, and the doctrines of Rome were once more finding favour in England. The validity of the marriage was questioned, and in July 1540 it was declared by Parliament to be null and void.

At the top of the hill, a small wooden gate leads us out onto a broad grassy path; after a hundred yards we pass through a second gate and cross the drive to **Moundsmere Manor**. Pass the three-way 'bridleway' sign and, still keeping straight ahead, join the farm track that drops downhill beside a wooden post and rail fence. At the foot of the hill turn left onto a sunken, tree-lined track, with some good views of Moundsmere Manor to the left. Three hundred yards further on we turn right onto the byroad towards Bradley; crest the hill, drop down to the crossroads, and turn right once again.

Follow the lane for 400 yards, before forking left onto the

waymarked **Oxdrove Way** opposite Keeper's Cottage. The drove begins as it means to go on, tucked up between thick hedges that almost meet above the track – though for a brief quarter-mile we find ourselves following waymarks across the open fields of Preston Down. In just over a mile we cross the Preston Candover road, and a similar distance brings us suddenly out onto the manicured gravel drive fronting some lavish brick and flint houses on Chilton Down. Beyond the drive we cross an avenue of ancient yews, and scan the view towards Chilton Candover.

In the spring of 1928, correspondents from the nation's press converged near the far end of this avenue in great excitement. For the rector, the Rev. Gough, had made what the Morning Post *described as '... one of the most remarkable discoveries of recent years.'*

It had all started quietly enough. The parishes of Chilton Candover and Brown Candover were united during the nineteenth century, and in 1876 the church of St Nicholas at Chilton Candover had been pulled down. The old churchyard became neglected and overgrown, and Rev. Gough decided to tidy it up. In the course of his work he was talking to eighty-year-old William Spiers, who had lived in the village all his life. The old man poked at the ground, and remembered that as a boy he had kicked skulls around in '... a great old place underneath there.' The rector became curious and, helped by his son, began digging in the spot that old William had shown him. What the two men revealed was variously described by the press as an 'underground church' or a Norman crypt; there were even suggestions that the building may originally have been a temple to the Roman god Mithras. The discovery was featured on radio, in journals as diverse as The Times *and the* Children's Newspaper, *and in local papers from Chiswick to Yorkshire.*

A third of a mile beyond the avenue our way crosses two metalled roads in quick succession. We leave the **Oxdrove** at the next waymark, 400 yards further on, turning right onto the downhill track for the short mile back to **Brown Candover**. As the track swings first to the left, then back to the right, the sight of St Peter's church beckons us on the final stretch into the village.

Picturesque cottage at Broad Oak, near Odiham (Walk 5)

Watership Down on the Hampshire and Berkshire border (Walk 6)

The Wakes, home of early ecologist Gilbert White (1720–93) (Walk 14)

Walk 10 – Silchester Roman Town

Bramley and Silchester

Distance:	5½ miles (7 miles including a circuit of the walls)
Start/Finish:	Bramley railway station
Terrain:	Field-edge paths and country lanes; will be muddy after rain
Map:	OS Landranger sheet 175 OS Explorer sheets 144 & 159
Refreshments:	The Four Horseshoes or the Village Stores, West End Green The Bramley Inn, Bramley
Information:	Calleva Atrebatum Roman Town Trail leaflet from Tourist Information Centre, Old Town Hall, Market Place, Basingstoke: 01256 817618
	Large display in the Silchester Gallery, Museum of Reading, Blagrave Street, Reading: 0118 939 9800
	Tiny Calleva Museum at Silchester, ½ mile west of the Roman town

So many of our great cities are built on top of their Roman foundations that a deserted Roman town, lying half forgotten in the Hampshire fields six miles north of Basingstoke, is something rather special. Visitors can walk the complete circuit of the Roman walls, and visit the compact little amphitheatre at the north-east corner. Although the interior of the town is now farmland, the original street plan can still be seen in aerial photographs. In England, only Caistor and Wroxeter have survived to a similar extent, so it seems appropriate to visit Calleva Atrebatum like a pilgrim – on foot, and using the old Roman road.

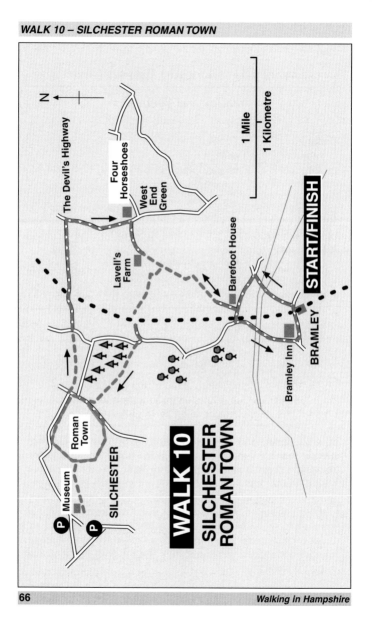

Catch the train to **Bramley** and head east from the level crossing, turning almost immediately left into Bramley Lane, an area of scattered modern housing. As we pass Bramley Primary School on the right, the pavement disappears, and we continue under the power lines to Holly Cross. Turn left here, signposted Silchester and Pamber Heath, by the charming old red-brick farmhouse with its scattered, tumbledown wooden barns and clay tile roofs.

The lane has wide grass verges, and the countryside is dotted with hedgerow trees. Turn right 100 yards before the railway bridge, where a little wooden footpath sign points up the rough track leading to Holly Cross Farm. After a couple of hundred yards we come to a collection of corrugated farm buildings on the right, and a little brick farmhouse on the left. The lane veers left into the farmhouse, but we carry straight on through a wicket gate, following the hedgerow trees on the left of the field.

There's an opening in the hedge after about 150 yards, but carry straight on, with the hedgerow still on our left. The modern path runs alongside an old overgrown sunken track, still clearly visible between the double line of hedgerow. At the top of this field we go through a gap straight ahead, and turn left at the wooden footpath sign in the hedge. After 50 yards a small black and white footpath sign wedged into the hedge points us across the open field on the right, just to the left of a small radio mast in the distance.

Once across the field, we come to the corner of a little copse where the two-way sign shows a path straight ahead, as well as one to the left. Turn left here and follow the path for about a quarter of a mile, now with the woodland on the right and the field on our left. When the field edge swings away left, keep straight on through a gap in the hedge into the next field, still keeping the hedge on the right.

At the end of this field, about 100 yards before the power line, we come to a rough farm track. Zigzag right and then left, following the wooden footpath sign onto a metalled farm road that leads us under the power lines. Continue under the railway line and a second set of power lines and, after a couple of hundred yards, follow the lane around to the left and join Clappers Farm Road. Turn right at the little duck pond, past the attractive red-brick and timber buildings of Clappers Farm itself. Here the lane swings to the right; but our way lies over the stile directly ahead, by the little wooden footpath sign.

Almost at once the path crosses Silchester Brook on a substantial iron-railed bridge, and a second stile leads out into a grassy field.

It's worth a short diversion on the left here, where there's open access to a thirteenth-century moat and fishpond. Here too lies an eighteenth-century water meadow, where willow trees were grown to produce cricket bats. Under a conservation plan the moat will be carefully preserved, and the grassland maintained by light grazing. The sluices, ditches and channels will be restored, and water will once again flow from the Silchester Brook to 'drown' the fields and enrich the lush spring grass.

Returning to the stile at the end of the footbridge, we follow the post and wire fence along the edge of North Copse until, at the very end, we turn briefly left onto a tarmac track. In 20 yards turn right, now with a little duck pond on the left, and follow the grassy track straight ahead; soon we get our first glimpse of the white painted walls and low shingled spire of Silchester church. Duck through a little scrubby area and follow the line of hedgerow trees on the left-hand side of the field. Almost at the road, the path veers to the right, and the impressive stone walls of **Silchester Roman town** heave into view. Look out for a narrow gap in the hedge just here, leading down out of the field and onto the road opposite the small church car park.

Although the building contains some reused Roman materials, the charming little church of St Mary the Virgin is not mentioned in Domesday book. It may have been built around 1167, and the addition of the north aisle in about 1230 completed the basic ground plan that we see today. Nevertheless, there have been many alterations and additions in the intervening centuries, culminating in Rector Fiennes' major restoration during the 1870s.

After visiting the church, turn north as far as the junction with Wall Lane for a look around the neat little Roman amphitheatre. Then we turn left for about 50 yards, and nip over two stiles on the left in quick succession. Here we climb up onto the ramparts inside the Roman wall, and follow them around to the right.

On the opposite side of the town from St Mary's church, a ½ mile track leads down to the tiny **Calleva museum**. Around the south side of the town, the easiest path initially follows the outside of the walls as far as the South Gate. Here, where the Roman road marched proudly south towards Winchester, the walls still stand up to 20 feet high and are quite well preserved. A faced stone entrance gives a good idea of how the gate must once have looked, and here we have the choice of continuing at the lower level, or climbing back up onto the ramparts inside the Roman wall.

Back at the church, continue up Church Lane towards the amphitheatre. Near the junction with Wall Lane, just by the letter box, a little wooden footpath sign points to the right and we take a cross-field path heading for the woods on the horizon. This path runs close to the line of the old Roman road to London and, walking across the open fields with little in the way of immediate landmarks, you can almost hear the tramp, tramp, tramp of the legion's boots.

On the far side of the field we nip over the stile, and take the metalled lane straight ahead. The lane climbs quite steeply and crosses the railway on an iron-girder bridge. Half a mile beyond the railway turn right at the T junction and drop down towards **West End Green**, with its attractive little duck pond on the right. Our way turns off to the right at the wooden footpath sign by the pond, towards **Lavell's Farm**; but a few yards further on, either the **Four Horseshoes** or the Village Stores with its small tearoom offer a welcome refreshment break.

The track bends to the left, passing the radio mast which we saw in the distance on the outward leg. Approaching the farm buildings, the track swings back to the right, but we slip up onto the edge of the field on the left. Now we keep the hedgerow on our right for 200 yards, to the corner of the little copse where we rejoin our outward route as far as the bottom of Holly Cross Farm lane.

Turn right across the railway bridge, then immediately left at the road junction. Return to the village past the nicely converted Stocks Barns on the right, and bear round to the left towards the **Bramley Inn**, an attractive red-brick and tile-hung free house standing just to the west of the railway station.

Walk 11 – Border Country

Petersfield

Distance:	9 miles
Start:	Petersfield railway station
Finish:	Rowland's Castle railway station
Terrain:	Cross-country paths; will be muddy after rain
Parking:	At both the railway stations
Map:	OS Landranger sheet 197 OS Explorer sheet 120 & 133
Refreshments:	The Five Bells, Buriton Queen Elizabeth Country Park visitor's centre (10.00am–5.30pm daily, April–October) The Red Lion, Chalton The George, Finchdean The Coffee Pot, Rowland's Castle
Information:	Queen Elizabeth Country Park visitor's centre: 023 9259 5040

By English standards, Petersfield is a relatively modern place. At the time of the Norman Conquest the area was part of the manor of Mapledurham, given by King William to his wife, Queen Matilda. It may have been Matilda who founded the chapel of ease at 'St Peter's-in-the-field', to save worshippers a boggy two mile trek to the mother church at Buriton. Be that as it may, we can be reasonably sure that St Peter's church has been casting its shadow over the Market Square since Petersfield's charter was granted in the twelfth century. The market has been held twice weekly ever since and, in recent times, Petersfield has developed into a compact and attractive little country town.

Leaving the **railway station**, we make a bee-line down Lavant Street towards the town centre. Cross Charles Street, turn right at the T junction into Chapel Street, and follow the road around to the left into the Square. Passing William III's statue, the narrow St Peter's Road leads us out of the far corner of the Square and round towards Dragon Street, where we turn right.

Behind the small shopfront of 38 Dragon Street, Judy Sparrow opened Britain's first Bear Museum in 1984. Inside, Teddies of all shapes and sizes vie for our affection, and fashion-conscious bears can visit the gift shop to purchase new items for their wardrobe. The displays include bears dating back as far as 1905 – and there is, naturally, a Teddy Bears' picnic!

As we head out onto the **Causeway**, we're following the steps of those early Christians threading their way across the marsh. But it's drier here nowadays, and on the outskirts of the town we can lift our eyes to look out for an unmade lane on the left.

Here we join the Hangers Way, following it as it zigzags briefly through a caravan park, then crossing the first of several double stiles and pushing out into open country. The noise of the town dies away as we cross two fields separated by another double stile, and join a broad grassy track that leads us down to the foot of a gentle slope. Cross the brook by the plank bridge, nip over the stile, and follow the brook as it flows beside the left-hand edge of the next field. At the end of the field a wooded coomb opens up to the left, guarded by a plank bridge and double stile. Jump over here, and join the grassy path that clings to the valley side, winding through a secret landscape until, half a mile further on, the pretty back gardens of Buriton jostle for position across the valley. Turn right at the stile, and follow the Hangers Way down into **Buriton** village.

In Saxon times Buriton formed part of the manor of Maple-durham. The original church, centre of a large parish of some 6000 acres, was mentioned in the Domesday survey of 1086; but the present building is a twelfth-century Norman replacement. Standing foursquare above their reflection in the village pond, these enduring flint walls remained the mother church to Petersfield until as recently as 1886.

Across the pond from the church, the Hangers Way leaves Buriton

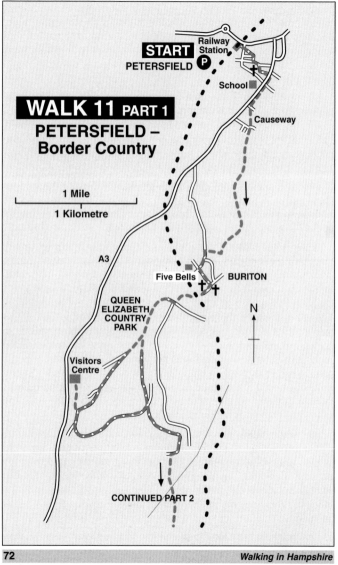

START
PETERSFIELD

Railway Station

School

Causeway

WALK 11 PART 1
PETERSFIELD –
Border Country

1 Mile

1 Kilometre

A3

Five Bells

BURITON

N

QUEEN
ELIZABETH
COUNTRY
PARK

Visitors
Centre

CONTINUED PART 2

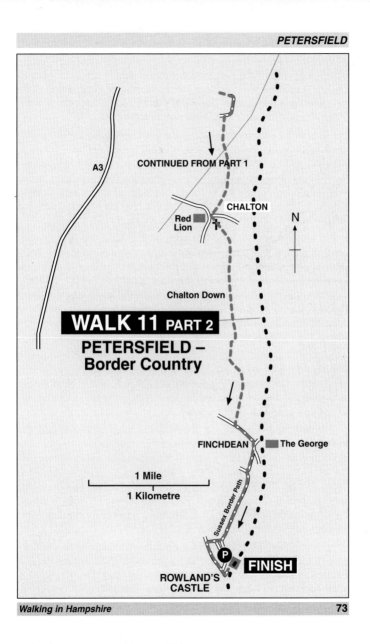

A3

CONTINUED FROM PART 1

CHALTON

Red
Lion

N

Chalton Down

WALK 11 PART 2

**PETERSFIELD –
Border Country**

FINCHDEAN   The George

1 Mile

1 Kilometre

Sussex Border Path

P

FINISH

ROWLAND'S
CASTLE

along South Lane. The surface soon deteriorates, and we burrow under a brick railway arch before winding gently upwards through old chalk quarries to a complex junction of minor roads at the northeast corner of the **Queen Elizabeth Country Park**. Cross over here, and follow the broad gravel bridleway into the park.

The track bears steadily left and climbs uphill; behind us and to the left, the wide views give a sense of achievement and a taste of the walk in front. The track divides at the crest of the hill, and here we have a choice. Fork right, following the South Downs Way, to the well-equipped **Visitor's Centre** at the start of the Staunton Way. Alternatively, we can press on, bearing left along the short cut that keeps close to the park's eastern boundary.

In either case, we leave the park on the Staunton Way, *named after Sir George Staunton, who bought his Hampshire estate in 1820 after a distinguished career with the East India Company.* After a couple of miles in the woods, there's a sense of release as we nip over the stile near the information board at the south-east corner of the park, and head south across open farmland to Chalton. A mile of easy, downhill walking takes us under the power lines, where we join the farm track leading to the village green.

*This tiny hamlet of around seventy souls is little more than a church and pub which, with good reason, stand head to head across the green. For, beneath its enormous thatch and jettied upper windows, the **Red Lion** started life in 1147 as a live-in workshop for the builders of St Michael's church.*

Directly opposite the pub, the Staunton Way heads out over the close-cropped churchyard turf, whose secret is given away by a notice declaring 'sheep at work'! Keep left through the churchyard, leave by the stile, and follow the path to a second stile. Here, where three paths diverge across the field, the Staunton Way follows the rightmost path over the broad back of **Chalton Down**. Near the summit, look back over your right shoulder for a glimpse of the fifteenth-century mill on Windmill Hill.

Beyond the crest of the hill we drop down under the power lines to a stile. Bear right here, and zigzag round a small thicket. Soon a bridleway crosses our path, we skirt a small patch of mainly yew woodland on our right, and follow the signpost down to meet the

Chalton–Finchdean road. Jump the stile, and turn left along the road for the few hundred yards into **Finchdean**.

Here, The **George** offers determined drinkers their last opportunity for a pint this side of Rowland's Castle. The rest of us turn right, following the road for a hundred yards before taking the right hand fork for a short, sharp climb. A couple of hundred yards further on, as the road swings to the right, we follow the Staunton Way as it levels off to the left. This broad, grassy lane soon passes a gate and narrows to a path across open fields.

At length, a small wooden gate leads us left and then right onto a farm track, passing the pretty Wellsworth Farm on the right-hand side. Soon, the track becomes a metalled road, and we're hemmed in by suburban houses. Pass a couple of turnings on the left and, at the T junction, turn left down Bowes Hill.

An easy third of a mile takes us down into **Rowland's Castle**. There was indeed a castle here in Norman times, though most of what once remained now lies buried beneath the railway. The station, for trains back to Petersfield, is tucked away on our left, just before the railway bridge. But, with a bit of decent planning, we'll just have time for tea and some delicious cakes at The Coffee Pot, around the corner on the right!

Walk 12 – War and Peace

The Meon Valley

Distance:	12 miles
Start/Finish:	The Shoe pub, in Exton village
Terrain:	Farm and disused railway tracks, also cross-field paths with frequent stiles. Will be muddy when wet
Parking:	Informal parking on spacious verge at grid ref SU617212
Map:	OS Landranger sheets 185 and 196 OS Explorer sheet 119 (Compass useful for one short stretch)
Refreshments:	The Bat and Ball at Broadhalfpenny Down. At least one pub in all the other villages along the route.
Information:	Winchester Tourist Information: 01962 840500 Meon Valley Railway Walk: 023 9246 2879

Wind on the hill, the smack of willow on a leather ball – these are the peaceful sounds drifting across the Meon valley nowadays. Yet it wasn't always so – for the little river takes its name from the Meonwaras, Jutish invaders who settled the area in pre-Saxon times. In our own century, war cast a shadow over the valley again when its little railway played a small part in the D-Day preparations.

Take the narrow lane south-east from the **Shoe** and, after a couple of hundred yards, go straight over the A32 crossroads towards Meonvale Farm. Pass Prospect Cottage on the right, then bear right at the next junction as far as the dismantled railway bridge. Just beyond the bridge, a path on the right leads us up onto the old embankment, and we turn south onto the Meon Valley Railway Path.

For the next mile and a quarter the old line is pleasantly shaded with ash, sycamore and horse chestnut, and there are attractive glimpses of the valley beyond the track. Our route crosses the B2150 on an overbridge at **Droxford**, but it's worth dropping down the embankment and walking the few yards up Station Road to the letter box.

Here, a plaque records the railway's special contribution to victory in the last war. The line carried little in the way of special traffic, apart from evacuees travelling from the coastal towns to the relative security of the countryside. But early in June 1944, Sir Winston Churchill and his War Cabinet met with other Allied leaders in a special train at Droxford station, to plan the imminent invasion of Europe. The station building is now a private house, but it can be seen from Station Road.

Back on the railway, the path follows a diversion around the station house, and a further mile brings us to the steel underbridge at **Soberton**. Walk under the bridge, and turn immediately left up the steps, joining the **Wayfarer's Walk** as it follows the lane past the White Lion and St Peter's church, and down School Hill to the Parish Hall. Go straight over the crossroads and, after a couple of hundred yards, follow the Wayfarer's Walk as it forks off to the left, just past Westdown Cottage. The stiff climb up onto Soberton Down is rewarded by wide views to Old Winchester Hill in the north, and the Isle of Wight in the south. The black and white *WW* waymarks now lead us across pasture and cornfields, through woodlands and over stiles. We pass East Hoe Manor, and drop down towards the B2150 with well-tended flower and vegetable gardens on either side. Turn right onto the main road, and follow it as far as the junction with West Street, where we turn left into **Hambledon** village.

Perhaps best known for its cricketing connections, Hambledon is also the home of the English wine industry. Hambledon Vineyard was founded during the 1950s by Major-General Sir Guy Salisbury-Jones, and the vines still grow on the southern slope of Windmill Down. Nestling beneath them, on the north side of West Street, is the Church of St Peter and St Paul. The original eleventh-century building has

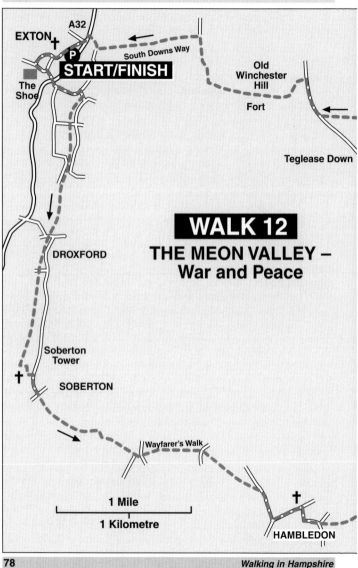

EXTON

A32

South Downs Way

P

START/FINISH

The Shoe

Old Winchester Hill

Fort

Teglease Down

DROXFORD

WALK 12
THE MEON VALLEY –
War and Peace

Soberton Tower

SOBERTON

Wayfarer's Walk

1 Mile

1 Kilometre

HAMBLEDON

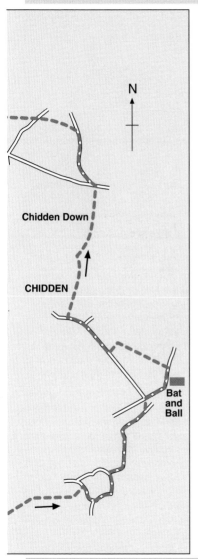

been much extended over the centuries, but some Saxon stonework can still be seen within the present structure.

Our route, still signposted Wayfarer's Walk, now turns to the right up the lane just before the George Hotel. At the bend in the lane, where the main line of the Wayfarer's Walk heads south over the mountainous flank of Speltham Down, we bear left and follow the lane as it climbs steadily upwards. This is one of several circular routes based on the Wayfarer's Walk, and the next 3 miles are waymarked *WW-C*.

At the top of the lane, we carry straight on up the drive of Rose Cottage, next to a little wooden footpath signpost. In a matter of yards the drive becomes a country path, leading in turn to a farm road. Just before the farmyard, the footpath swings to the right, skirts the farm buildings, and comes to a stile. Nip over here, and follow the line of electricity posts across the fields towards Glidden Farm.

Now cross a further four stiles; the last one, beside a farm gate, leads onto a farm track which ends by a pond on our right. We turn right here, onto

The Bat and Ball pub at Broadhalfpenny Down

another track, then keep around to our left until the track meets a metalled lane. Turn right, and follow the lane past the pretty Scotland Cottage, where it reverts to a farm track. Just after the old Ordnance Survey trig point on the left the lane swings right, skirting the fir trees on our left, and emerges to give us a fine view of HMS Mercury on the far side of the valley. A hundred yards beyond the trees, jump the stile on the left and drop down towards the road from Hambledon to Clanfield. Turn right, and cover the last 300 yards to the crossroads.

And so we arrive at the cradle of the English summer game, described in the Gentleman's Magazine *for 1791 as '... the famous cricket ground, called Broadhalfpenny, at the foot of which is a two-mile course for horse matches. The inhabitants of this town have long been famous cricketers, and a club here is not afraid to challenge all England.' A massive stone memorial opposite the Bat and Ball pub bears witness to the men of Hambledon Cricket Club who wielded their curved bats on the greensward between 1750 and 1787. The pub, built in 1730, still makes an attractive refreshment stop, and the Broadhalfpenny Brigands continue the cricketing tradition on this most hallowed of grounds.*

Turn left at the **Bat and Ball**, and follow Hyden Farm Lane for 200 yards to the little wooden footpath sign on the left. Nip over the stile here, and follow the field edge as far as the woods on the left. Cross a second stile, and follow the edge of the woods to the gate out onto the lane.

Here we say goodbye to the *WW-C* waymarks, and turn right up the lane towards **Chidden**. Half a mile further on, a wooden footpath sign points our way right, towards a belt of woodland that swings in from the left. At the corner of the field, dodge into the woods and turn right up the muddy trackway by the wooden footpath sign. In a little over a hundred yards the track bursts out of the woods through a metal gate, and we follow it between wire fences as far as the road from Warnford to HMS Mercury.

Cross over here, and take the lane towards Coombe, drifting gently down around the steep bluff of **Teglease Down**. At the foot of the hill turn left through the wicket gate, and follow the footpath as it bears gently left, keeping the wire fence on the right. In half a mile we zigzag left and right across the lane, before trekking west across a trackless field towards the summit of **Old Winchester Hill**. Few places in lowland Britain justify carrying a compass, but this is one of them. You can manage without one, but that little magnetic needle is a definite asset.

The National Nature Reserve on Old Winchester Hill is one of the jewels in Hampshire's crown. This is one of just a few scattered places on the South Downs where acid loving species such as heathers grow alongside more typical chalkland vegetation. Skylarks pour out their liquid song above the hill fort, and butterflies such as the marbled white and chalkhill blue flitter across the paths. Look out for fragrant orchids and round-headed rampion, and the old yew woodlands clinging to the scarp slope. The hill is crowned by an Iron Age fort, and from the summit there are spectacular views in every direction.

Here we pick up the **South Downs Way** and follow it off the hill, passing under the Meon Valley railway walk. A third of a mile beyond the old railway bridge we turn right, over the attractive iron-railed footbridge that sweeps low across the River Meon. Cross the A32 with care, and follow the back lane for the last half mile to the **Shoe** in **Exton** village.

Walk 13 – The American Connection

West Meon

Distance:	5 miles
Start/Finish:	West Meon
Terrain:	Farm and disused railway tracks, also cross-field paths. May be muddy when wet
Parking:	Plenty of informal parking in the old station yard
Map:	OS Landranger sheet 185 OS Explorer sheet 132
Refreshments:	The Thomas Lord and The Red Lion, West Meon; The George and Falcon, Warnford; The Shoe, Exton
Information:	Winchester Tourist Information: 01962 840500 Meon Valley Railway Walk: 023 9246 2879

The departure of the Legions in AD410 brought more than four centuries of Roman imperial rule to an end. In southern Britain, the vacuum left by the Roman withdrawal was filled by invaders from Jutland, who used the Isle of Wight as a base for incursions onto the mainland. The Jutish Meonwara tribe settled in the coastal forests and pushed inland from Titchfield, giving their name to the Meon valley and its villages.

Christianity first reached the area in the late seventh century when, according to tradition, the exiled Northumbrian Bishop Wilfrid preached beneath an ancient yew tree in the centre of West Meon. The present church is more recent, having been designed by Sir Gilbert Scott and consecrated in 1846. If it looks familiar, you may be thinking of a likeness, for when Arnold Constable decided

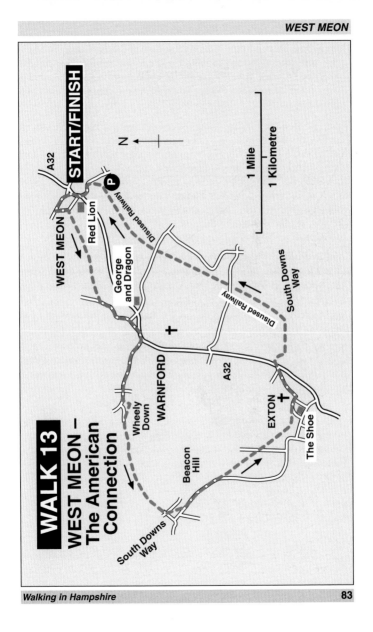

WALK 13
WEST MEON –
The American
Connection

START/FINISH

A32

N

1 Mile
1 Kilometre

WEST MEON

Red Lion

P

Disused Railway

George
and Dragon

South Downs Way

Disused Railway

WARNFORD

A32

South Downs Way

Wheely
Down

Beacon Hill

EXTON

The Shoe

to build a church in the New York suburb of Mamaroneck, he and his wife toured Europe looking for a suitable model. They liked this one so much that they copied the design, and the Mamaroneck version of St John the Evangelist, West Meon, was completed in 1886!

From the **Red Lion** in the centre of the village head briefly north up the A32 towards Alton. In a matter of yards, turn left at the war memorial and walk up past the church. Two hundred yards further on turn left again into Floud Lane, and follow it down towards the attractive converted buildings at Court Farm Barns. Turn right at the bottom of the lane, where a wooden footpath sign points our way along the grassy field-edge track. Our route lies close to the 100 metre contour, and the nearby A32 hardly detracts from the pleasant, wooded views as we work our way down the valley towards **Warnford**.

We dodge through a narrow belt of trees into a second field and, on the far side of the field, a stile leads us out onto a narrow lane. Turn left here, and follow the lane for the last half mile into Warnford.

A little off our route, and approached through Warnford Park, the ruins of St John's House stand close by the church of Our Lady, Warnford. The house was an unusual example of a stone built hall, constructed around the turn of the twelfth and thirteenth centuries. It belonged to the de Port family, one of the great Hampshire landlords at the time of the Domesday survey, and the aisled hall was supported on stone pillars some 25 feet high. The church itself was founded by our old friend Bishop Wilfrid, and renovated by Adam de Port.

In Warnford we turn right, joining the A32 for a couple of hundred yards and passing Rose Lea Cottage before turning right again onto the back road towards Winchester. The road rises gently past the watercress beds, Hampshire Hogs Cricket Club and, finally, the Wheel Horse barns, all on the left-hand side. Just over half a mile from the main road, turn left at the wooden bridleway sign, and wind between the forge buildings onto a gravel track that climbs steadily towards **Wheely Down** and **Beacon Hill**. Soon the track zigzags right and left over a stile, and we continue our climb with close-cropped turf underfoot. This section is well waymarked, with plenty of opportunity to enjoy the lovely views across the Meon valley.

Towards the top of the hill the path runs alongside a finger of woodland on the left. After about a quarter of a mile the woods close in on both sides, and we dive straight in, emerging a few hundred yards further on at a small parking area amongst the trees. Swing left here, over a stile, and pick up the **South Downs Way** as it drops down the hill into Exton. To the right, there are clear views down the Meon valley to the Solent and the Isle of Wight. At last the path noses into **Exton** and joins the back road, where we turn left towards the church of St Peter and St Paul.

Like so many country churches, this one was largely rebuilt in Victorian times, and the occasion gives us a tantalising whiff of local scandal. In 1840 the MP for Salisbury, a certain W. Wyndham Esq, had presented a clock to the parishioners of Exton. But during the rebuilding in 1847 it was taken down and returned to him, '... the giver being disapproved of by the inhabitants.'

The road bends sharp left at the church, and we follow it for a quarter of a mile to the A32. Zigzag left and right across the busy main road, still following the **South Downs Way** as it crosses the River Meon by an attractive little footbridge. Across the river the path swings to the left and, after a third of a mile, arrives at the brick built arch of the Meon Valley Railway Walk. Here we nip up onto the embankment and follow the old line north, for two miles of pleasant, easy walking back to West Meon.

By the dawn of the twentieth century, the great network of trunk railways was largely complete. Expansion now depended on secondary routes, and the railway companies fought constant skirmishes to extend their territories at the expense of their competitors. In Hampshire, the Great Western had reached both Winchester and Basingstoke, and now had its sights on the south coast ports. To counter that ambition, the Waterloo-based London and South Western Railway promoted their own route between Basingstoke and Fareham, following the Meon Valley southwards from Alton.

Success came at a price. The Great Western were beaten off, but the L&SWR sank over half a million pounds in a project that was a commercial disaster. The line was built for speed, and though it opened with a single line of rails, the stations were lavish and earthworks constructed for double track. But the traffic simply didn't materialise, and the second line was never laid. The timetable was leisurely, and trains were sometimes delayed whilst the crews gathered wild mushrooms from the fields beside the track.

The line drifted through the inter-war years, and enjoyed its moment of glory in the run-up to D-Day (see Walk 12). But the route was an early casualty of post-war economies, and closed to both passengers and freight in 1955.

The railway walk ends at the site of the former West Meon station, where nature is steadily recolonising the once spacious layout. Drop down the station access road and turn left for the short walk back to the **Red Lion**.

Selborne Church (Walk 14)

Walk 14 – Gilbert White's Outdoor Laboratory

Selborne

Distance:	7¼ miles
Start/finish:	Selborne village centre
Terrain:	Woodland and field paths, bridleways and some brief stretches of road. The Zigzag Path is a fairly energetic climb.
Parking:	Free car park behind the Selborne Arms
Map:	OS Landranger sheet 186
	OS Explorer sheet 133
Refreshments:	Tearooms in Selborne and refreshments at the Wakes Museum. The Selborne Arms and the Queen's Hotel in Selborne; the Rose & Crown at Upper Farringdon
Information:	Tourist Information Centre, Alton: 01420 88448
	Tourist Information Centre, Petersfield: 01730 268829
	The Wakes Museum, Selborne: 01420 511275

This glorious woodland walk takes us between the mighty beech trees of Selborne Hanger and then across delightful open country to peaceful Selborne Common. The village of Selborne is famous as the home of the eighteenth-century naturalist Gilbert White whose book The Natural History of Selborne *brings many visitors and nature lovers to the village every year. With good reason. In the words of the National Trust guide, 'the area is the mecca of naturalists and nature lovers, the living green outdoor laboratory of Gilbert White.' There are a number of different editions of White's classic, first published in 1788, and over the years it has been translated into French, Danish, Swedish and Japanese. His original manuscript was sold at Christie's in 1980 for £100,000.*

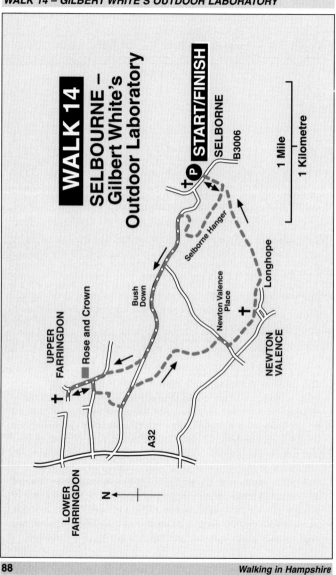

WALK 14

SELBOURNE –
Gilbert White's
Outdoor Laboratory

START/FINISH

SELBORNE

B3006

1 Mile

1 Kilometre

Selborne Hanger

Longhope

Bush Down

Newton Valence Place

NEWTON VALENCE

Rose and Crown

UPPER FARRINGDON

LOWER FARRINGDON

A32

N

White was an extremely gifted man and in his time he was a curate, a naturalist and an Oxford don. After school he went to Oxford and became a Fellow and Dean of Oriel but later returned to his beloved Selborne to become curate. Nothing gave White greater pleasure than strolling these secluded paths and leafy glades in search of the local flora and fauna. Undeniably, he was a pioneer in the field of English natural history.

Before beginning the walk proper, take a stroll through **Selborne**. There is much to catch the eye. Heading down the B3006, we soon come to the old butcher's shop and slaughter house on the right. *In 1756 White recorded in his journal, 'Planted four limes in the butcher's yard to hide the sight of blood and filth from the windows.' Two of the original four trees still survive. The slaughter house also remains, its windows reinforced with iron. The butcher's shop traded until the First World War.*

On the left is the Wakes Museum, where White lived. The house includes furnished rooms and delicately embroidered bed hangings. Part of the museum is devoted to the naturalist and explorer Francis Oates, and his nephew Captain Lawrence Oates, who joined the fateful Antarctic expedition in 1911. Opposite is **Selborne church**.

Inside St Mary's are reminders of Gilbert White, including a window dedicated to him, which depicts St Francis of Assisi feeding the birds. The window has 64 birds in it. The church is about seven centuries old but the site for the original one was given by the wife of Edward the Confessor. There is also a chapel with a flight of steps dating back 700 years, which originally had pews on them designed for children. Now they have coffin stones which were removed here from a priory.

Return to the car park and follow the path signposted to **Selborne Hanger**, pausing to brace ourselves for the Zigzag Path which leads us up to the beautiful beech-clad hill above.

Selborne Hanger was described by Gilbert White as 'a vast hill of chalk rising 300 feet above the village, and... divided into a sheep down, the high wood, and a long hanging wood called a hanger. The cover of this eminence is altogether beech, the most lovely of all forest trees...'

The Zigzag Path was cut by White and his brother in 1753. It was intended as a short cut to the top of the hill. The path allows thousands of people to visit this beautiful spot every year and to do so by a clever and novel means. There is a seat at the top where we can pause to rest and admire the scene.

The Wakes, home of Rev Gilbert White (1720-93), England's first ecologist

With our back to the seat, we turn left and go up several steps, veering right when the path forks. Now we follow the clear path through the woodland, with Selborne glimpsed to our right through a thick canopy of trees. The path gradually begins to descend and eventually reaches a junction with a track. Turn right and follow it between trees and hedgerows. Pass a stile on the right and continue to the road. Bear left and follow the lane as it twists and turns through the countryside; at one point we pass through a tunnel of trees before turning sharp left. We leave the road at this point and go straight on along a bridleway. After about 100 yards go through a gate on the left and then head diagonally right across the field to a gateway in the trees. Once through the opening, we cross the next field by going obliquely left up the slope. Pass several trees and look for a track running into the woods.

We follow the bridleway between lines of oak and beech trees. The ground can be extremely wet and muddy along here. Pass under some pylons and bear right when you reach a path for **Upper Farringdon**. Follow the path across open ground to the road. While we are in the village, we can stroll along to Massey's Folly, located near the church.

One of Hampshire's most eccentric edifices, this ornate folly has been a village school, church hall and general meeting place in its time. It was in 1870 that the then village rector, the Rev. Thomas Hackett Massey, himself one of Hampshire's more colourful characters, decided to build in the village. However, he chose a red-brick house which was completely at odds with everything else in Upper Farringdon. Some people have commented that its exuberant gothic design was inspired by St Pancras railway station in London. The scarlet terracotta panels are especially striking. The folly boasts 17 bedrooms and it is thought Massey may have had a theological college in mind. Others suggested it was intended to be a tearoom for the London–Portsmouth railway. Rev. Massey also helped build the folly, employing the services of an unknown bricklayer. However, it took them both 30 years to finish it. Massey was liable to bouts of bizarre, unpredictable behaviour and it was not uncommon for him to demolish parts of the building that did not meet with his liking. It seems his congregation grew ever smaller during the construction work. This was mainly due to Massey's fondness for preaching hell-

fire and damnation every week. Finally, only the bricklayer and a washerwoman attended his services. Massey died in 1939 and is buried near the church porch.

Make for the **Rose & Crown** and continue in a westerly direction through the village, turning left opposite Brownings Orchard. Follow the bridleway through the trees and when it bends right, cross a stile, go up the slope and across several stiles to reach a junction of paths. Now we head straight on across open farmland, descending the slope to reach a stile in the bottom left-hand corner of the field. Turn left and follow the outline of a path along the field boundary. Head for woodland on the horizon and eventually we reach a footpath sign in the field corner. Bear right and follow the clear track all the way to the road. Turn right and pass Reed Cottage.

Our walk soon brings us to an octagonal lodge on the left. At this point we follow the signposted footpath through the parkland of **Newton Valence Place** and eventually reach a wrought-iron kissing gate in the top boundary. Cross the drive leading to the house and continue on the footpath as it veers half-right to a gate. Follow the path alongside a laurel and holly hedge and soon we come to a drive. Turn left and enter Newton Valence churchyard.

Gilbert White was curate here for a time. The magnificent yew standing in the churchyard is about seven yards round; the yew grows in such profusion in this county that it is known as the 'Hampshire weed'. St Mary's is thirteenth century and was restored in 1871.

On leaving the churchyard, we keep to the left of St Mary's, along an avenue of yews and then through a copse. Soon we cross a stile and bear right. A hard tennis court edges into view along here. Cross another stile and then head diagonally right across the field to a further stile. A few steps beyond it we reach a junction of paths on Selborne Common. During the nineteenth century cricket was played here and cattle once grazed among the trees and the grassy glades. The common is now in the care of the National Trust. Head straight across and take the path signposted to **Selborne** via Church Path. Follow the path through glorious woodland and eventually we arrive at a junction. Turn right and walk along to the seat at the top of the Zigzag Path. From here we retrace our steps down to the car park.

Walk 15 – In Search of Sheep Droves

Bentworth

Distance:	6½ miles
Start/Finish:	**Bentworth church**
Terrain:	**Field paths, tracks, byways and several stretches of minor road**
Parking:	**Limited spaces at Bentworth church and elsewhere in the village**
Map:	**OS Landranger sheet 185** **OS Explorer sheet 144**
Refreshments:	**The Star and the Sun at Bentworth; the Yew Tree at Lower Wield**
Information:	**Alton Tourist Information: 01420 88448**

We follow in the steps of sheep drovers along ancient tracks and byways on this very pleasant circular route in the Candover valley south of Basingstoke. Part of our walk takes in the Oxdrove Way, a 25 mile cross-country riding route which was probably used in Saxon times for driving sheep and cattle. The track cuts through the Hampshire countryside and here the scene is a timeless rural picture of fields, hedgerows and copses.

We start our walk at **Bentworth**, a peaceful village which was once a royal manor owned by the Bishop of Rouen. The churchyard contains a tree grafted from the Holy Thorn at Glastonbury.

From the church we walk along to the junction and keep left, turning right just beyond a thatched cottage to cross the green. The village looks as pretty as a picture in high summer and when the sun is shining it is very pleasant to sit in the shade of a tree on the green and admire the tranquil scene. Make for a stile near the seat, head down to the bottom left-hand corner of the paddock, cross a second stile and head diagonally across the field, aiming for a break in the

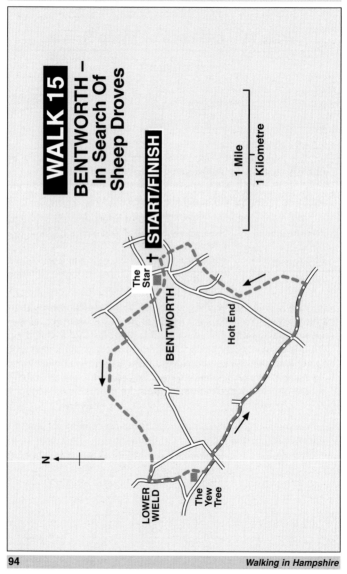

WALK 15
BENTWORTH –
In Search Of
Sheep Droves

+ START/FINISH

The Star

BENTWORTH

Holt End

LOWER WIELD

The Yew Tree

N

1 Mile
1 Kilometre

fence. Go obliquely right in the next field to the road. At this point we cross over and follow the path along the left boundary of a field, passing through a gap in the hedgerow by some galvanised gates.

Turn left and follow the wide grassy track, bearing right at the next junction. Head up the straight track to some trees and look for a footpath sign on the left. Head diagonally across the field to a gap in the trees, near the right-hand corner. We keep right now, picking our way beneath the branches to a junction of tracks by a pond on the right. The Oxdrove Way crosses our route here. We turn left to follow the byway between trees. Follow the track beyond a break in the woodland, pass a stile on the left and then look for a gap also on the left. If the track is very wet and muddy, it is easier to follow the parallel path along the field boundaries. Keep to the right of some corrugated barns and join a metalled road.

Walk along to the next junction and turn left, signposted Upper Wield. Follow the lane through **Lower Wield** and when it bends sharp right, we go straight ahead over a stile. Keep to the right of a derelict barn and pass between trees and bushes to the edge of a field. Follow the path ahead to a stile in the far boundary and go out to the road.

To visit the **Yew Tree** turn right; to continue the walk turn left. Follow the road to the next junction and bear left, signposted Bentworth. Take the next track on the right and another track merges from the right after about half a mile. Avoid the turning and continue on a section of the Oxdrove Way to the next main junction. Bear right here, avoiding a turning sharp right, and follow the track to the next road. We cross over here and follow the metalled lane which serves several properties. Pass Broomhill and turn immediately left to join a byway, following the track to the road at **Holt End**.

Turn right and pass the 30 mile speed limit sign. Bear sharp right at the footpath sign and turn left at the waymark. Cross a stile and follow the edge of a garden. Continue along a field boundary, avoiding a stile leading to the cricket ground, and cross two stiles. Negotiate two more stiles, either side of a drive, and follow the field edge to two further stiles, with a track in between. Skirt the field edge to a stile and foot-path sign. Turn left here and go up the field to another stile, then continue on an enclosed path to the road. To finish, go straight over and follow the path through the trees, back to the church at **Bentworth**.

Walk 16 – Buckland Rings

Lymington

Distance:	4½ miles
Start/Finish:	Lymington Town Station
Terrain:	Mostly all-weather surfaces, but short section of bridleway may be muddy after rain
Parking:	Public car parks just off Lymington High Street
Map:	OS Outdoor Leisure 22, New Forest (recommended)
	OS Landranger sheet 196
Refreshments:	The Toll House Inn, Buckland; wide choice in town centre (open all year)
Information:	Lymington: 01590-672422 (closed winter)
	Lyndhurst: 023 8028 2269 (open all year)

The fast expresses that sweep majestically through the wooded Inclosures and purple heaths of the New Forest pause for breath in Brockenhurst, where the little branch line train waits patiently to carry us down to Lymington. Here, the extensive Saturday market rivals any in Hampshire, with colourful stalls selling everything from garden tools and foam rubber to greetings cards and fast food.

Early in the nineteenth century, attempts were being made to introduce universal education. By the 1830s, grants had become available towards school building projects and, in 1834, Mrs St Ann Barbe gave £220 to buy the site '... for a school for poor children of the parish of Lymington.' The school was subsequently built on land in New Lane (now New Street, just off the High Street) and it opened in January 1836. It survived several extensions and changes over more than a century and a half, before the Infants School

Gilbert White country between Selborne and Petersfield (Walk 14)

The top of the Zigzag Path, overlooking Selborne (Walk 14)

The walk near Bentworth (Walk 15)

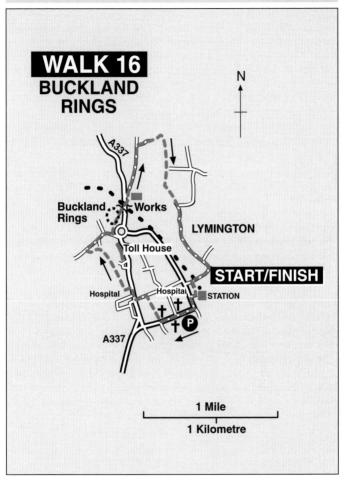

WALK 16
BUCKLAND RINGS

N

A337

Buckland Rings

Works

LYMINGTON

Toll House

START/FINISH

Hospital

Hospital

STATION

A337

1 Mile

1 Kilometre

finally moved out in 1992. The old school building was saved by the Lymington Museum Trust, and now houses the charming Visitor Centre and St Barbe Museum.

Turn left at the top of **Station** Street, and in a couple of minutes bear round to the right, into High Street. Near the top of the High Street stands the town's oldest building, St Thomas' church, with its domed cupola and south tower. Inside, substantial galleries panelled with plaques recording the building's history surround three sides of the nave. Follow the path through the churchyard, and out onto Avenue Road. Turn left here, then right at the traffic lights, onto Southampton Road. Just beyond the hospital, zigzag left and right through Kings Road into Park Avenue; at the top, a little gravelled footpath leads our feet away from the town towards the red-brick buildings of Buckland Manor Farm.

The path loops left and right around the farm buildings, then joins the gravelled track through the farmyard and out onto Sway Road. Cross the road, nip through the wicket gate, and follow the field edge on the right for a couple of hundred yards, to a second gate on the right-hand side. You can leave the field here for the 100-yard walk to the **Toll House Inn** and Buckland Heritage Centre. Alternatively, turn left across **Buckland Rings** Iron Age fort, emerging onto the A337 near the railway bridge at the north-east corner of the site.

Beside the Toll House Inn, the Heritage Centre occupies the charming little Toll House Cottage. Tolls were charged on the Lymington to Totton road between 1765 and 1850, and the Toll House was built as the home of the tollgate keeper in around 1789. The ground floor of this compact little museum houses fascinating displays covering the 250-year history of the local licensed trade. Upstairs, drawings and photographs tell the story of nearby Buckland Rings, and there are good maps of the paths across the site. The museum is open during the pub's lunchtime hours (winter excepted). What better excuse do you need?

A few steps lead us down out of the Buckland Rings site and onto the A337. Cross over, and turn left under the railway before taking the right-hand fork up tree-shaded Boldre Lane. After half a mile, just past Shallowmead Nurseries, dive off to the right down a little sunken lane, and cross the infant River Lymington by a white-railed foot-bridge. Fifty yards further on, we turn right through a wicket gate and follow the lush bridleway that leads down through the Reedbeds Nature Reserve.

Please keep dogs on the lead through this 80-acre reserve, owned by the Hampshire Wildlife Trust. Otters live in the river, and the site is home to some 300 species of moths and butterflies. Look out, too, for swallows and housemartins, as well as the rarer Cetti's Warbler and Bearded Tit.

When our path leaves the reserve, we keep straight on along the quiet Undershore lane for half a mile. At the B3054 junction keep straight ahead, following the road as it sweeps to the right and crosses the Lymington River. But for the traffic on the bridge, this would be a peaceful scene; there are reedbeds upstream, and gaily painted hulls float on the wide lagoon to our left. Beyond the river, cross the level crossing and turn immediately left down Waterloo Road to return to **Lymington** station.

Walk 17 – Coasting Along

Lymington and the Solent

Distance:	3½ miles
Start/Finish:	Lymington Town Station
Terrain:	Mostly all-weather surfaces
Parking:	Public car parks just off Lymington High Street
Map:	OS Outdoor Leisure 22, New Forest (recommended)
	OS Landranger sheet 196
Refreshments:	Wide choice in town centre (open all year)
Information:	Lymington: 01590-672422 (closed winter)
	Lyndhurst: 023 8028 2269 (open all year)

Sea salt production was once a major industry in the Lymington area, and around 160 salt pans once lined the coast between Lymington and Hurst. In the years between 1694 and 1825 salt was generally taxed at five shillings (25p) a bushel, returning no less than £55,000 to the Exchequer in 1755. At the start of the last century the area produced some 6000 tons of salt annually, valued at one shilling (5p) a bushel. By this time the tax had doubled, and it was soon increased to fifteen shillings (75p) a bushel to help finance the wars with France. This punitive taxation added to the problems of the local industry, which was facing increased competition from the Cheshire salt mines. Cheshire salt was easily transported by canal, and on the expanding railway network. When the railway eventually reached Lymington in 1858, it was too late; by 1845, this 700-year old industry was at an end.

Turn left at the top of **Station** Street and, in a couple of minutes, turn left down the cobbled Quay Hill. Bear around to the right at the bottom, towards the old harbour, and keep straight on along Bath

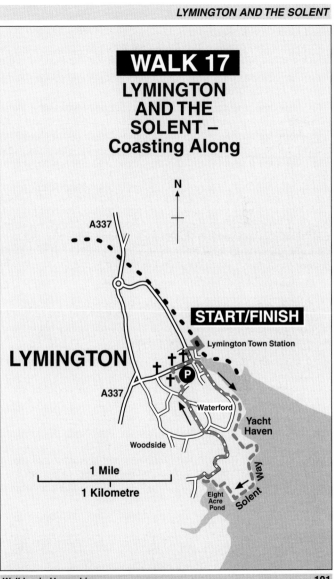

WALK 17

LYMINGTON AND THE SOLENT – Coasting Along

N

A337

START/FINISH

Lymington Town Station

LYMINGTON

A337

Waterford

Yacht Haven

Woodside

Solent Way

1 Mile

1 Kilometre

Eight Acre Pond

Road to the recreation ground. Here we cut across to our left, join the riverside path, and pick up the **Solent Way** – pausing, perhaps, to watch the Isle of Wight ferry glide listlessly down the river. Pass the Royal Lymington Yacht Club and the lifeboat station, keeping the open-air swimming pool on the right.

Follow the signposted Solent Way through the marina boat park, across the saltings, and up onto the sea wall. A broad gravel path tops these sinuous coastal defences, and throughout the next mile we can relax and take in the wide views across the Solent to Hurst Castle and the Isle of Wight. On the landward side, a profusion of seabirds wheel over the old salt works.

Leave the sea wall at **Eight Acre Pond**, home of the Salterns Sailing Club, and keep hard right into the meandering little Normandy Lane. After three-quarters of a mile we cross All Saints Road, walk up Broad Lane, and turn right into Grove Road. Almost at once keep left into Grove Pastures, and follow the narrow alley leading out into High Street.

As we turn right into the High Street, the granite obelisk to Admiral Sir Harry Burrard Neale dominates the trees on Walhampton Hill dead ahead. Time for a little refreshment, perhaps? There's plenty of choice here, before turning left at the foot of the High Street and retracing our outward route to the station.

Walk 18 – Hampshire's Amazing Mizmaze

Whitsbury Village

Distance:	10 miles
Start/Finish:	The Cartwheel pub, in Whitsbury village
Terrain:	Bridleways, field paths and downland tracks
Parking:	Informal parking in Whitsbury or at the Cartwheel. Please get permission from the landlord.
Map:	OS Landranger sheet 184 OS Explorer sheet 130
Refreshments:	The Cartwheel at Whitsbury and the Rose & Thistle at Rockbourne; there is a picnic area at the Rockbourne Roman villa.
Information:	Fordingbridge Tourist Information: 01425 654560 (closed in winter) Breamore House: 01725 512468

We head for western Hampshire's remote downland country on this spectacular walk, in search of a fascinating antiquity imbued with a strong sense of the distant past. Concealed by an isolated grove of yew trees high on the downs, and fenced off to protect it from erosion, the turf-cut Mizmaze is one of the county's most enigmatic curiosities. But this is not a maze in the traditional sense, more a labyrinth where all paths curve in a symmetrical pattern to a central mound. Its precise age is unknown but mazes of this kind are often associated with penitential rituals. Only by getting away from the well-trodden tourist trails can we really appreciate the true character of these downs. With their prehistoric earthworks and ancient relics, we can savour something of their timeless atmosphere and real sense of history.

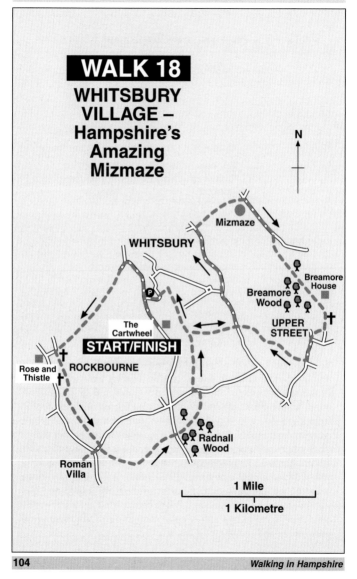

WALK 18

WHITSBURY VILLAGE – Hampshire's Amazing Mizmaze

N

Mizmaze

WHITSBURY

Breamore House

Breamore Wood

UPPER STREET

The Cartwheel

START/FINISH

Rose and Thistle

ROCKBOURNE

Radnall Wood

Roman Villa

1 Mile

1 Kilometre

We turn right from the **Cartwheel** inn at Whitsbury and walk up the street, passing a stud on the left. A glance at the map reveals evidence of castle ditches over to the right at this point. The original camp was part of a network of defences built to guard this lonely chalk country from the threat of Saxon attack. Pass the entrance to Whitsbury Manor Stud, then swing left and left again by some white fencing as the road bends right. Follow the bridleway through a white gate and walk between copper beech trees. Go through several gates and follow the path down under the trees to two more gates. Now we head across the field to join a track running down to the buildings of Manor Farm. Keep to the right of them and follow the lane into **Rockbourne**, passing a turning on the left for the medieval church.

St Andrew's contains monuments to the Coote family, including Lieutenant-General Sir Eyre Coote, an eighteenth-century military hero who persuaded Clive of India to launch an attack at Plessey, resulting in victory for the British. A 100ft monument, commemorating Lieutenant-General Coote's achievements in the field of battle, was erected on the downs to the south of Rockbourne in 1828.

After touring the village, make for the path to the right of the churchyard. Pass two footpaths on the right and then turn right immediately beyond a stile. Go through a galvanised gate and head diagonally down the field to a second gate. Avoid the double gates on the right and follow the track, keeping a fence on the right, to the next waymark. Follow the field edge to a stile and maintain the same direction, the field boundary now on our left. On reaching a house, negotiate two stiles and cross the road by the entrance to Marsh Farm. Cross three fields by keeping close to the right-hand edge, then join a path between fence and hedge to a stile.

Turn right and right again at the next junction to visit **Rockbourne Villa**. *This Roman gem was discovered by a local farmer in 1942 and includes mosaic floors and a baths complex. Over seventy rooms have been uncovered over the years, confirming the villa as one of the largest Roman farmsteads of its kind in Britain. Among other fascinating features, the underfloor heating systems of the bath house can be seen when the site is open to the public.*

To continue the walk we go straight over the road and follow the track, passing through a tunnel of trees to a junction. Continue for

Breamore House

several yards, then bear left up the steep bank to a field edge. Keeping woodland on the left, we soon head out across the field. On reaching a track we turn right, then left at the next footpath. Follow the path through some trees, keeping left at a waymark. Skirt a private garden and turn right at the road. Bear left after a few steps, opposite Brookheath House, and follow a woodland bridleway. Avoid a right-hand path and bear left at the next road.

Turn right at the junction for Whitsbury, avoid a bridleway running off sharp right, and continue for a few yards to a bridleway running off half-right. Follow the right of way through the wood and eventually we reach a junction of tracks. Turn sharp right and head down through the trees to a field. Continue down to a gate, bear left and follow the track. Keep right at the turning for Lower Farm and continue for more than half a mile to a junction of tracks with a stile and gate on the right. Bear right and follow the field edge, continuing ahead on a track between trees and hedgerow to a corrugated barn on a track bend.

Go straight on through the trees and keep right at the next junction, following the grassy track to a stile. Turn right and approach some woodland, then swing right on the grassy path. Veer right at the fork and walk alongside the trees to the entrance to the **Mizmaze**. Discover this lonely place at any time of the year and it is impossible to deny its curious, almost eerie atmosphere. We could spend hours dwelling on its precise origin, picturing how it was designed and exactly who created it, but time marches on and we still have some way to go to reach the end of the walk. Head down the grassy slope and along the track, then veer right at the next junction and follow the track through **Breamore Wood** to **Breamore House**.

A splendid Elizabethan manor house, Breamore contains many fine artefacts acquired by ten generations. The house was damaged by fire in 1856 but retains the front façade, as well as two striking fireplaces and a staircase. The nearby Countryside Museum includes examples of a farm worker's cottage, a blacksmith's forge and a cider barn – among other features.

From Breamore House it is an easy amble down the main drive to the road. Now we turn right and follow the road round the left bend. Soon we bear right into Rookery Lane, keeping ahead on a sunken path. Veer right at the fork and continue through the trees. Cross a stile and follow the gulley and field edge to a gate. Turn right for several steps, then bear left at a gate, retracing our steps up the field and through the wood. Follow the track alongside paddocks and turn left at a bungalow and outbuildings. Bear left at the next junction and swing right at Whitsbury church. Go down through the churchyard to a kissing gate, then head down the field to a second gate. Descend to the road and turn right for the **Cartwheel**.

Walk 19 – Castleman's Corkscrew

Through the New Forest from Ashurst to Brockenhurst

Distance:	8 miles
Start:	Ashurst (New Forest) railway station (formerly known as Lyndhurst Road station)
Finish:	Brockenhurst railway station
Terrain:	Forest rides and tracks; will be muddy after rain
Parking:	Car parks at both stations
Maps:	OS Landranger sheet 196
	OS Outdoor Leisure 22
Refreshments:	New Forest Hotel, Ashurst; Beaulieu Hotel, Beaulieu Road; several pubs and tea shops in Brockenhurst
Information:	New Forest Visitor Centre, Lyndhurst: 023 8028 3914

The Saxon kings were already hunting in this part of south-west Hampshire before the Norman conquest. But in 1079 William I designated the New Forest a Royal hunting park, and subjected it to strict forest laws. This was not a good time for the peasants who – on pain of death – were forbidden to enclose their crops, take timber for building, or catch game for their tables. Nevertheless they were granted a number of rights, some of which have endured into modern times. Commoners could gather firewood (the right of estovers) or cut turf for fuel (turbary) and they were also allowed to pasture their animals on the open forest. Around 5000 ponies and cattle still graze the forest to this day, and during the autumn pigs are turned out to forage for acorns and beech mast (the right of pannage).

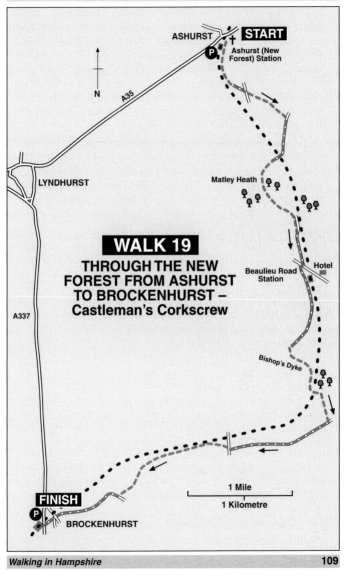

ASHURST

START

Ashurst (New
Forest) Station

P

↑
N

A35

LYNDHURST

Matley Heath

WALK 19

THROUGH THE NEW
FOREST FROM ASHURST
TO BROCKENHURST –
Castleman's Corkscrew

Beaulieu Road
Station

Hotel

A337

Bishop's Dyke

1 Mile

1 Kilometre

FINISH

P

BROCKENHURST

Over the centuries the Crown's interest in the Forest turned from the sporting to the strategic, and vast areas of woodland were 'inclosed' to provide timber for the Royal Navy's ships. Today the pendulum has swung back, and over seven million people now visit the New Forest every year for leisure and recreation. Traffic on the major routes west of Southampton frequently grinds to a halt on summer weekends, and trying to park in popular centres like Lyndhurst and Beaulieu isn't the best way to begin a day in the country.

But you don't have to get caught up in all that; take the train to Ashurst, and follow this delightful route across the full width of the Forest park to Brockenhurst station. The walk includes a wide variety of scenery, and although it rarely strays far from the railway, the line never dominates its wild, secluded character.

Leave **Ashurst station** by the gravel path at the northern end of platform two, and follow the railway for about 100 yards. Beyond the wooden pedestrian gate bear right, away from the A35 road, and double back through a second gate into a long narrow field of close-cropped turf fringed with trees and bushes on both sides. For almost half a mile our route keeps close to the railway, crossing three small sleeper footbridges before coming to a set of wooden gates leading onto the gravelled forest ride straight ahead.

Beyond the gates we follow the ride into the dense mixed woodland. After 200 yards it crosses another gravelled ride, continuing as a rough track with tussocky grass underfoot. We keep straight on at the grassy 'crossroads' in Deerleap Inclosure, climbing gently to a five-way junction where we take the second ride on the right. Now we enter an area of more open, coniferous woodland; pleasant, easy walking in the pine-scented air.

Seven hundred yards further on, the ride doubles back on itself at a set of wooden gates. We leave it here, pass through the gates, and head out across the railway on a white railed footbridge some hundred yards to our right. Soon we cross the infant Beaulieu River on a small brick bridge, and our track bears gently to the left across the wide expanse of **Matley Heath**.

Follow the thinly-marked path towards a finger of woodland to

Walkers near Denny Lodge in the New Forest

the south, where two footbridges and a short gravelled causeway carry us safely across Matley Bog and back out onto open heathland. Bear gently left towards the railway and, after a short half mile, join the sandy track some 20 yards west of the railway fence. The track keeps company with the railway as far as the B3056 road, where weary travellers can turn left for **Beaulieu Road station** and the inviting 'Stables' bar and restaurant at the **Beaulieu Hotel**.

This section of railway was promoted by a Wimborne solicitor, Charles Castleman, and opened in 1847. It formed part of a meandering line between Southampton and Dorchester that also served Brockenhurst, Ringwood and – inevitably – Wimborne. The slow, roundabout route earned the railway its nickname of 'Castleman's Corkscrew' and, in 1888, it was bypassed by the present main line via Christchurch and Bournemouth. The Ringwood section began a long, steady decline that ended with closure during the mid-1960s; parts of the line have been taken over for road improvements, and Holmsley station has survived as a popular tearoom.

We cross the B3056 at the little Shatterford car park and head out over the open heathland, still following a sandy track some 50 yards west of the railway. Half a mile further on the track bears to the right over a gravel causeway and wooden footbridge, and parts company from the railway. This is a boggy area, and two further footbridges lead us close to some attractive pools fringed with silver birch.

A hundred yards beyond the second bridge we leave the gravel track and bear left onto a grassy woodland path that follows the **Bishop's Dyke** along the fringe of the woods to our right. After half a mile's walk through these ancient deciduous woodlands, the railway draws in from our left; the path climbs towards it, and crosses the tracks on an ugly, mesh-walled bridge. We drop down from the bridge between white railings, and turn right through a five-bar gate onto a green forest ride through young beech woodland.

The beech woods soon give way to conifers and, after about a quarter of a mile, we turn right at a forest crossroads onto a waymarked gravel ride. A mile's easy walking brings us to a cattle grid and T junction at waymark number 40. Turn right here, keeping an eye out for the occasional car, and follow the gravel road for about 100 yards. Just as the road begins to climb towards the railway bridge, veer off across the grass to the left and pick up the informal woodland path that runs close to the railway boundary. This path is well used by animals, and can be boggy in places!

The railway is our guide for the next half mile, and we pass an attractive brick and tile cottage near the next bridge. Keep straight on through lightly wooded grazing land, with the railway still 50 to 100 yards on the right. Two hundred yards beyond the cottage, look out for a small brick arch under the railway; our way lies 60 yards to the left, through a little wooden gate into New Copse Inclosure. The green woodland path is now better defined; we cross a small brook on a wooden bridge, and pull slowly away from the railway through attractive mixed woodland.

After 400 yards we come to a T junction, and turn left onto a broad woodland ride. Two hundred yards further on a gravel track swings in from the left; keep straight ahead, now with gravel underfoot, for a further 100 yards. Here we fork right onto a grassy ride which carries us 300 yards to a small wooden gate leading out onto the B3055 road. Turn right for 100 yards, then left, crossing a cattle grid and a white railed bridge over the Lymington River.

To our left lies Brockenhurst Park, established during the late eighteenth century by Edward Morant. Morant's new estate combined Watcombe and Brockenhurst Farms, and he created a parkland setting by removing the hedgerows and turning over the fields to pasture. He retained the mature oak trees, some of which have survived to support a number of rare lichens. Morant's parkland is currently being restored to its original eighteenth-century appearance.

In just under a mile we pass the imposing North Lodge and cross the busy A337 to finish our walk at **Brockenhurst** station.

Walk 20 – Exploring Conan Doyle Country

Lyndhurst and Minstead

Distance:	11 miles
Start/Finish:	Swan Green, Lyndhurst
Terrain:	Mostly level forest paths and tracks. Some stretches of road. The forest can be very wet underfoot, particularly in winter.
Parking:	Swan Green free car park
Map:	OS Landranger sheets 195 & 196
	OS Outdoor Leisure 22
Refreshments:	The Swan, Swan Green. The Trusty Servant at Minstead is open all day in summer. Cream teas are available at Acres Down Farm midway round the walk.
Information:	New Forest Museum and Visitor Centre, Lyndhurst: 023 8028 2269
	Furzey Gardens: 023 8081 2464

Following leafy paths and tracks, this lengthy woodland walk takes us to the heart of William the Conqueror's Nova Foresta. Along the way we stumble on a curious relic of the First World War and visit colourful Furzey Gardens, open daily throughout the year. In the tree-shaded corner of a quiet country churchyard we find the graves of Sir Arthur Conan Doyle and his wife who lived locally.

From **Swan Green** car park, go diagonally across the green, making for the bottom corner near the main road. About 50 yards before reaching it, we cross a ditch and then head for a wide path running up **Lyndhurst Hill** between trees and banks of undergrowth. The main A35 is parallel on the left. Pass over a cross-track and continue between hollies, oak and beech trees. The track begins to descend quite steeply now and on the level ground it cuts between trees and banks of bracken. Further on we can see the outline of **Allum House**

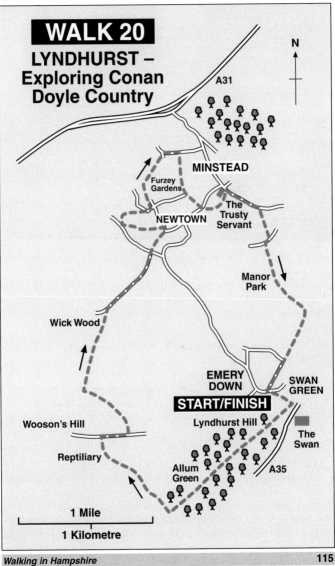

WALK 20

LYNDHURST –
Exploring Conan
Doyle Country

N

A31

MINSTEAD

Furzey
Gardens

The
Trusty
Servant

NEWTOWN

Manor
Park

Wick Wood

EMERY
DOWN

SWAN
GREEN

START/FINISH

Lyndhurst Hill

The
Swan

Wooson's Hill

Allum
Green

A35

Reptiliary

1 Mile

1 Kilometre

Swan Green near Lyndhurst

and its walled garden up ahead. *The house was once the home of the Fenwick family who donated the hospital of the same name at Lyndhurst.* The hospital features later in our walk.

We continue alongside a high brick wall, passing Caister Cottage and Corner Cottage. As the track bends left, swing right and head for a seat amid the trees. Beyond it continue on the clear grass path which gradually curves right. At the next major junction, bear left and descend the hill. Merge with another path and continue. Cross a bridge over a stream and bear right at the junction. Follow the firm track and soon we reach a cottage on the right. Just beyond it is the entrance to the **Reptiliary** at Holidays Hill Inclosure. *The site, established in 1972, helps small creatures such as the sand lizard to survive by providing a breeding reserve.*

Go through the gate leading to the Reptiliary. After looking round the site walk towards the car park for a few yards, passing a sign – 'we hope you enjoyed your visit' – and then pass through the gate on the right to join a track. Follow it through the Inclosure and eventually we come to a junction. Bear right and soon we reach the road.

Turn right and walk down to the Portuguese Fireplace, of all things, located amid the trees beside the road.

It may be somewhat unusual to stumble upon such a distinctive antiquity in this lovely wooded setting, but to local residents the Portuguese Fireplace, neglected and worn by the passage of time, is one of the New Forest's best-known and long-established landmarks. The fireplace stands on the site of a hutted camp occupied by a Portuguese Army Unit in the First World War. The New Forest played a vital role in the war effort and the local workforce was greatly assisted by the Unit, whose members helped produce timber in local lumber camps. The flint fireplace comes from the old cookhouse and serves as a memorial to the men who lived and worked here.

Continue along the road and bear left to join a clear track, sign-posted Millyford Bridge. Pass through the barrier and keep to the left of the parking area. Follow the track through the forest, pass over the

Highland Water, one of many New Forest streams, and go through a gate to continue between endless rows of trees. Cross another foot-bridge, then, after about 150 yards, we reach a crossroads. Take the track on the right and follow it between bracken and felled trees. Go through a wooden gate and continue as the track narrows to a path. Pass under the boughs of beech trees and continue on the clear path. Cross a footbridge, go through

*The Trusty Servant,
Minstead*

Conan Doyle's grave at Minstead

a clearing and soon we reach a stony track on a bend.

Go straight on and pass the car park for Acres Down. Join a lane at Acres Down Farm and follow it down to the ford. Continue between fields to pass Robins Bush Farm, then, at the road junction, go straight over to follow a lane. Turn left at the next junction by a telephone box and post box and bear left after a few yards to join a waymarked bridleway running into the forest. Follow the secluded path through a tunnel of trees and between banks of bracken. Eventually we reach the road. Go forward for several yards, then turn right to follow the stony track, keeping left at the fork. Pass the entrance to a house called Skymers. As the track bends right by a cream-coloured house, go straight ahead into the wood. After a few yards, we reach a junction. Bear sharp right here and follow the track down to a bend in the road.

Take the waymarked path on the left and follow it between hedges and fencing. Drop down to the corner of a field where there is a foot-bridge. Cross a tree-fringed pasture to a stile. Once over it, bear right and head down through the trees to a footbridge and section of board-walk. Veer right at the waymarked junction, cross another little foot-bridge, go on up to join a track and follow it to the entrance to **Furzey Gardens**. *As well as 8 acres of informal landscape, there is also a sixteenth-century cottage and a gallery selling the work of local craftsmen. The gardens are open daily throughout the year.*

On leaving the gardens, turn right and walk down the lane. Take the first turning on the right and follow the lane to the ford at **Newtown**. At the junction turn left, then right (no through road) and take the public footpath running through the wood. Soon it skirts **Minstead** church to reach the lychgate entrance where we can see a stand for resting coffins. Passing through the churchyard, we find the final resting place of Sir Arthur Conan Doyle and his wife. *Conan Doyle, who died at Crowborough in Sussex and was reburied here in the 1950s, lived at nearby Bignell Wood, north of the A31, and featured Minstead in his book* The White Company.

Walk down the road to the centre of the village. The **Trusty Servant** is on the left. Note the interesting pub sign which explains the inn's name. It is a copy of an original picture belonging to Winchester College. Bear right and walk along the road. Pass the entrance to Park Farm and just beyond it swing right to follow a lane to Williams Hill (no through road). On reaching the farm, go straight on along a waymarked track. Cross the Fleet Water and then veer left to reach the road. Turn right and follow the road until we see a path on the left, just before a house and beside a fallen tree. Take the path and after a few yards it curves to the right. Pass through a woodland glade, keeping to its right-hand edge. Soon we reach a stream. Beyond it swing right and then veer right at the fork at the top of the bank. Shortly we emerge from the trees to skirt the edge of a clearing for a few yards. Continue through the next burst of woodland and look for an extensive network of tree roots underfoot.

Pass a gate and stile and continue between carpets of invasive bracken, cursed by many farmers and landowners because it is so prolific and difficult to destroy. Keep left at the fork, then right at the next one, pass over a grassy cross-track and continue to a green at Bunker's Hill. The source of the River Beaulieu is near here. Turn right by some cottages to join the road. Follow it beside the entrance to Fenwick Hospital and continue all the way to the next junction. Bear left and then immediately left again to join a bridleway. Follow the stony track beside houses and laurel hedges. The track soon narrows to a path and runs on for some time, eventually reaching the road. Go along to the junction, opposite a church, and turn left. Follow the pavement down to the car park at **Swan Green**.

Walk 21 – Gateway to the World

Southampton

Distance:	3½ miles
Start/finish:	Ocean Village, Southampton
Terrain:	Pavements, parks and city walls
Parking:	Spaces at Ocean Village
Information	Leisure & Visitor Centre: 023 8022 1106.
	Guided walking tours with a Blue Badge
	Guide: 023 8086 8401
Map:	A good street map of Southampton
	OS Landranger sheet 196
	OS Outdoor Leisure 22

Think of Southampton and we tend to think of passenger liners, freight traffic and ferries. For 500 years it was one of England's leading ports, synonymous with shipbuilding and the golden age of ocean-going travel. However, as our fascinating heritage trail reveals, there is much more to this city than its sprawling docks and bustling waterfront.

Before beginning the walk proper, have a look at the SS Shieldhall which is permanently berthed at **Ocean Village**. Launched in 1955, it was built for use as a treated sewage disposal vessel, but don't let that put you off! This fully operational steamship offers a fascinating insight into day to day life at sea. Ocean Village is one of Southampton's most recent marina developments and attracts over two million visitors a year. Replacing the old Princess Alexandra Dock, the site consists of waterfront restaurants, bars and nightclubs and is also a venue for important international yachting events.

On leaving Ocean Village, we go straight across at the main road junction into Canute Road, turning right for the Hall of Aviation. This entertaining attraction is a fitting memorial to the achievements of R. J. Mitchell who designed the famous Spitfire fighter aircraft. Here we can

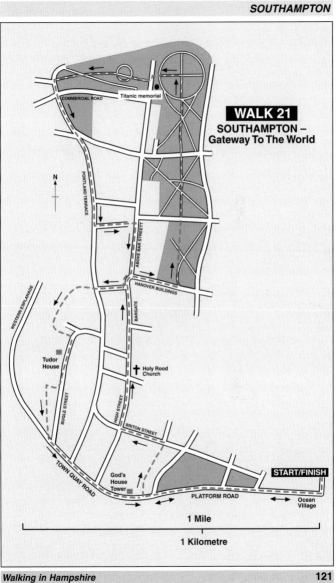

COMMERCIAL ROAD

Titanic memorial

WALK 21

SOUTHAMPTON –
Gateway To The World

N

PORTLAND TERRACE

ABOVE BAR STREET

HANOVER BUILDINGS

WESTERN ESPLANADE

BARGATE

Tudor
House

✝ Holy Rood
Church

BUGLE STREET

HIGH STREET

BRITON STREET

TOWN QUAY ROAD

START/FINISH

God's
House
Tower

PLATFORM ROAD

Ocean
Village

1 Mile

1 Kilometre

also climb up to the flight deck of the legendary Sandringham flying-boat around which the hall was built. The inside of the flying-boat is reminiscent of a first-class railway carriage, a classic reminder of the great days of luxury travel. Southampton Water was where these wonderful flying machines used to take off and land, a centre for early experimental flying and later a base for long-distance flights. The Sandringham seen in the museum took five days to reach South Africa.

Before resuming the route of the walk, take a stroll down the street, heading towards the Royal Albert Hotel and look for the Edward VII post box, a charming relic of the early twentieth century. Return to Canute Road and pass the South Western Railway Headquarters and Canute Chambers, which became the offices of the White Star Titanic line in 1907. On the left are the premises of the Wilts & Dorset Bank, established in 1835. On the right are the remains of the old Terminus station, which was opened in 1840 and is still regarded as a wonderful example of classic railway station architecture. The station was designed by Sir William Tite in an Italianate style with a ground floor colonnade. Terminus station was the city's main station until the opening of Central station. Adjacent to it is the former South Western Hotel, formerly the offices of BBC South and Radio Solent, which opened in 1872. Today, the building consists of luxury apartments. By obtaining permission from the security officer (weekends only), we can turn left here at Dock Gate 4 and stroll down to the little quayside memorial which marks the spot where the Titanic was berthed prior to her ill-fated maiden voyage in April 1912.

Return to the main road and walk through Queen's Park, passing the memorial to Major-General Charles George Gordon of the Royal Engineers. A soldier, administrator and philanthropist, Gordon was born at Woolwich in 1833 and killed at Khartoum in 1885. Continue along the road to reach the Platform Tavern – a hostelry with a difference. The pub, which was badly damaged during the air raids of the Second World War, is built against the old town wall which dates back to about 1350. Part of the wall can be seen inside, its stonework exposed to show its original state. High tides used to drench this defence until the eastern quay was built in 1830.

On leaving the pub, we turn left for several steps to begin the next stage of our trail – a walk into history along the remains of

Southampton's walls, taking us round the medieval town of Hampton and visiting many interesting buildings and landmarks en route. As we begin, we can pause for a few moments to have a look at the fifteenth-century **God's House Tower**, originally part of the south-east gate of the old town and one of the earliest artillery fortifications in Europe. The tower itself was built to protect the sluice gates which controlled the flow of water into the town moat. A ditch ran alongside the building until the 1850s, intended to link Southampton with the Andover canal and the River Test. There were once seven gates into the old walled town. Walk the walls today and the remains of five can be seen.

Follow the town wall, passing some striking tiled murals, and on reaching the British Telecom building we turn left along Briton Street. Bear right and follow the High Street, passing the ornate frontage of the old Post Office. Nextdoor to it is Junnes, an Indian restaurant. Look at the striking tiled design of the upper floors and the medieval merchant ship decorating the top. Our next objective is the ruined church of Holy Rood, erected in 1320 and damaged by enemy bombing on the night of 13 November 1940. Known for centuries as the 'church of the sailors', the ruins have thankfully been preserved by the people of the city as a memorial and garden of rest dedicated to those who served in the Merchant Navy and lost their lives at sea. There is also a memorial to the stewards, sailors and firemen who perished in the Titanic disaster.

Now we make for **Bargate**, one of the finest medieval gateways in the country, dating back to the late twelfth century. Up until the 1930s specially designed trams travelled through Bargate, with dome-shaped tops to fit the arch. The adjoining walls and buildings were subsequently destroyed so that traffic bypassed Bargate. Turn right here and walk down beside Houndwell Park to the roundabout. In the midst of noisy traffic, surrounded by flora and fauna, is a monument erected to William Chamberlayne, one-time MP for Southampton who gave the large cast-iron pillars needed to support gas lights in the city.

We cross over two roads on our stroll through East Park, making for the statue of Richard Andrews, a nineteenth-century coach-builder who was five times mayor of Southampton. The statue was unveiled in 1860, a year after his death. Turn left and walk along to the **Titanic memorial**, recalling the engineer-officers who 'showed their high conception of duty and heroism by remaining at their posts.' At this point we start to head down the High Street, passing the city's

Bargate in Southampton

awesome cenotaph designed by Edwin Lutyens. Cut through Watts Park behind it, pausing for a moment or two to study the sizeable monument to Isaac Watts, the famous hymn-writer who was a native of Southampton. The city's civic buildings and their famous soaring tower can be seen now. Pass the modern BBC headquarters and go over Marlands Road to reach Portland Terrace, its elegant Regency design and wrought iron balconies recalling Southampton's days as a fashionable spa town and resort.

Turn right and walk along the busy High Street, returning to **Bargate**. Bear right and make for the town wall again. Soon we reach Arundel Tower and Catchcold Tower, upon which there was an anti-aircraft gun for much of the Second World War. Heading south we come to the remains of the old castle and the site of the earliest fortifications for the ancient port. Evidence suggests there may have been a quay here, in the days when seawater reached this far inland. Castle Water Gate, as it is known, may well have had wooden, detachable steps running down to the quayside.

Further on we come to Pilgrims Gate, followed by Blue Anchor Lane. Here, we leave the old wall and make for the **Tudor House** overlooking St Michael's Square. This striking timber-framed building dates back to about 1500 and features some fascinating photographs of Southampton in previous years. Have a look at the Tudor garden which occupies a delightful, hidden corner of the city, then head south along Bugle Street and turn right for Westgate. Henry V marched his army through here on their way to Agincourt. Westgate is one of the finest and best preserved of these remaining fortifications. The portcullis was removed in 1744. Adjacent to Westgate is the Tudor Merchant Hall, moved from St Michael's Square to its present site in 1634. From here we make for the waterfront and the Wool House, now a maritime museum which explains in fascinating detail Southampton's role as one of the world's great ports. Nearby is the Mayflower memorial, which commemorates the sailing of the Pilgrim Fathers in 1620, and across the road is the crumbling Royal Pier, damaged by fire in the 1980s. Originally opened in 1833, this was once the largest pier in the south of England. From here it is a breezy hike along Town Quay to Ocean Village, keeping the waterfront over on our right.

Walk 22 – 'Pompey': Britain's Island City

Portsmouth

Distance:	3 miles – excluding detours
Start/Finish:	Portsmouth & Southsea railway station
Terrain:	Urban streets, squares and parks
Parking:	Plenty of car parks in the city centre but expect to pay
Map:	A good street map of Portsmouth is recommended for the walk.
	Alternatively use OS Landranger sheet 196 or OS Explorer sheet 119.
Refreshments:	Plenty of inns, hotels and cafés in Portsmouth and on the route of the walk
Information:	The Hard: 023 9282 6722
	Clarence Esplanade: 023 9283 2464
	Civic Offices Information Desk: 023 9283 4092

Portsmouth is unique as Britain's only island city. Affectionately known as 'Pompey' to seamen and footballers alike, Portsmouth evolved over the years into the south of England's largest and most important naval base, playing a key role in the defence of the British Empire and synonymous with Nelson's victory at Trafalgar. Those glory days may have gone but Portsmouth still retains its vital link with the sea, evoking images of England's fleets which have sailed from here to victory and defeat. The city's character is divided into two distinct categories. The heart of Portsmouth, characterised by its civic buildings and distinguished landmarks, has the air of a true city, while old Portsmouth, with its quaint houses and colourful waterfront, is totally different, more akin to a picturesque fishing port.

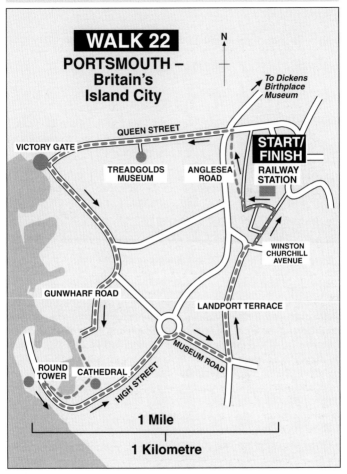

WALK 22

**PORTSMOUTH –
Britain's
Island City**

N

QUEEN STREET

VICTORY GATE

TREADGOLDS
MUSEUM

ANGLESEA
ROAD

START/
FINISH

To Dickens
Birthplace
Museum

RAILWAY
STATION

WINSTON
CHURCHILL
AVENUE

GUNWHARF ROAD

LANDPORT TERRACE

MUSEUM ROAD

ROUND
TOWER

CATHEDRAL

HIGH STREET

1 Mile

1 Kilometre

Before setting off in search of the city's hidden treasures, we can spend a few moments gazing up at the Victorian splendour that is Portsmouth and Southsea railway station. Its fine ironwork and imposing façade kindle memories of the golden age of steam travel.

Portsmouth Guildhall

With our back to the station building, we turn left and pass under the railway bridge. As the road bends left, go straight on by the entrance to the Mountbatten Gallery. There, looming into view, catching us by surprise in all its glory, is the pride of civic Portsmouth. The palatial Guildhall was opened in 1890 by the Prince of Wales for his mother Queen Victoria who, reputedly, was said to be anxious about the endless number of steps leading up to its grand entrance. However, the Guildhall's glittering centrepiece is its central tower which rises to over 200 feet and, despite encroaching office development, can still be seen from certain vantage points around the city. An imposing bronze statue of Victoria stands in front of the steps and the more modern local authority buildings opposite the Guildhall give the plaza a much-needed sense of balance.

Turn right into King Henry Street and ahead lies the Municipal College, now the University, its exuberant architecture dominating the street. Perched on top of the building is a distinctive weather-vane, appropriately in the form of a ship. Turn right between the

Ancient sheep droven, near Bentworth (Walk 15)

Walkers enjoying the forest scenery near Denny Lodge (Walk 19)

The New Forest, renowned for its tranquility and wildlife (Walk 19)

Bluebell time in Micheldever Wood (Walk 26)

Evening sunshine on Vernal Farm (Walk 27)

Peaceful fields near the site of the battle of Cheriton, 1644 (Walk 27)

Guildhall and the University entrance, where trains can be seen trundling in and out of the station. In its shadow, and echoing eerily to the hollow, tannoyed voice of the station announcer, stands one of the country's finest First World War memorials, guarded by the stone figures of two menacing machine-gunners. The humdrum activity of a city centre railway station going about its daily business versus the brutal reminders of war creates a curious juxtaposition. Suddenly discovering the cenotaph is unexpected, but the endless roll-call of names demonstrates the futility of it all.

From the cenotaph we enter Victoria Park, created when Portsmouth's defences were levelled in the 1870s to provide a much needed green lung at the heart of the city. Small but beautiful, this is a traditional city centre park with many mature trees, extensive flower gardens, a pets corner and an aviary. But this is no ordinary park. Virtually everywhere you look there are late nineteenth- century monuments, memorials and obelisks recalling long-forgotten wars of the British Empire. Look for the little Chinese Temple enclosing, of all things, an iron bell taken at the capture of the north-west fort of Taku in China in 1900 and brought home by the crew of HMS Orlando. The inscription on the bell reads, 'Come pleasant weather and gentle rain, the Empire happy, at peace again.'

Cross the park to Edinburgh Road and on reaching Portsmouth's striking Roman Catholic Cathedral we have a choice. A worthwhile detour involves a brisk walk up Alfred Road passing the red-brick late-Victorian church of St Agatha's. A bomb which fell in 1940 wrecked this deprived corner of Portsmouth and left the church a solitary symbol of hope at the heart of the devastated city. Regular worship continued here until St Agatha's was sold to the Royal Navy in the 1950s. Hampshire County Council acquired the building in the 1980s, carrying out a programme of restoration and landscape improvement with the aim of bringing the church back into public use again.

Turn left at the next roundabout and make for the **Dickens Birthplace Museum** in Old Commercial Road, to the right of the Oliver Twist pub. The most famous house in this street, which still has the remains of old tram lines, looks much the same today as it did when Charles Dickens was born here on 7 February 1812. His father was employed as a clerk in the Navy Pay Office and he and his wife Elizabeth rented the house, their first marital home, which is authentically furnished in the style of the period. With its cobbles, elegant houses and wrought-iron railings, the scene looks much like a film set from one of the author's own classics.

Return to the Roman Catholic Cathedral and turn right into **Queen Street**. Further down, we can pause to have a look at Bishop Street, a hidden side road which seems strangely quiet compared with the hurly-burly of Queen Street. Here, stepping back to Victorian England once again and far removed from the tourist trail, we find **Treadgolds Museum**, which, with its reconstructions of an ironmongers shop, stockroom and cart store, offers a unique slice of social and industrial history. The business was established in 1809 and traded until 1988. Return to the main route and make for **Victory Gate**.

It is here that visitors from every corner of the world begin their tour of Portsmouth's historic dockyard, discovering Britain's naval heritage and exploring 800 years of fascinating history brought to life by ships, museums and exhibitions. Allow plenty of time for a visit. There is so much to see. HMS Victory, the Mary Rose and the iron-clad nineteenth-century battleship Warrior are among the more obvious attractions.

Resuming the walk, follow The Hard towards Portsmouth Harbour station, which rises above the water on stilts. Now we amble alongside the old railway arches, a corner of Portsmouth that still evokes an air of the 1950s. This is the preserve of second-hand car dealers and unassuming café premises. However, we can expect some changes here soon. New public promenades are being created, opening up waterfront land closed to the public for centuries. Viewing terraces are also planned for major maritime events and, as part of the renaissance of Portsmouth Harbour, tall ship berths, massive water arches, cafés, bars and shops will enhance the bustling, colourful scene.

Follow **Gunwharf Road**, passing the Isle of Wight ferry terminal, and head along King James Quay to reach Portsmouth Point, a tiny peninsula at the mouth of Portsmouth Harbour. Outside the city walls and isolated from the rest of Portsmouth, aptly named Spice Island was once filled with sailors, prostitutes and press gangs. This was a major port importing exotic spices from around the world, its narrow streets bursting with life, danger and excitement. But there is much more to Spice Island than its cobbled lanes and rumbustious past. The **Round Tower** and neighbouring Square Tower squat on the old curtain wall, acting as a permanent reminder of Portsmouth's need to defend itself from enemy attack.

Stroll up the High Street, passing the old Garrison church, where Charles II married his Portuguese bride, Catherine of Braganza, in 1662. It was in this street in 1629 that the Duke of Buckingham met a violent end at the hands of an aggrieved soldier. On the left is Portsmouth **Cathedral**, without doubt one of the city's most striking buildings and originally a parish church built in honour of St Thomas a Becket. Damaged during the Civil War and later enlarged, it became a cathedral in 1927. Pass Portsmouth Grammar School and over to the left at the next roundabout is the Landport Gate, which dates back to 1698 and was originally one of the main entrances into Old Portsmouth.

Turn right into **Museum Road** and walk along to the City Museum and art gallery. Bear left into **Landport Terrace** and follow it into Hampshire Terrace, heading back towards the Guildhall. Once through the underpass, our attention is caught by an unusual-looking building on the right. Built in 1924, this former cinema was designed by an architect who had just returned to this country from the Khyber Pass. We are now in Guildhall Walk, where the accent is firmly on bars, clubs and pubs. On the left is the Theatre Royal, characterised by its exterior balcony on stylish cast-iron legs. Pass between the Guildhall and the statue of Queen Victoria and return to the station to end this fascinating and stimulating city trail.

Walk 23 – Sea Breezes

Titchfield and Fareham

Distance:	7 miles
Start/Finish:	The Square, Titchfield
Terrain:	Field paths and tracks; cliff top and canalside paths. Some stretches of road
Parking:	Free car park in Titchfield and further on-street parking
Map:	OS Landranger sheet 196 OS Explorer sheet 119
Refreshments:	Pubs in Titchfield including the Bugle, Coach & Horses and Queen's Head
Information:	Fareham Tourist Information: 01329 221342

Our delightful coastal walk starts in Titchfield, one of Hampshire's prettiest villages. Before starting, have a leisurely stroll through its charming streets of timber-framed cottages, pausing to admire the spired Norman church and various Georgian buildings. Titchfield was once an important port and market town with a thirteenth-century abbey which was pulled down by the first Earl of Southampton, Chancellor to Henry VIII. Titchfield's commercial prosperity was due in no small measure to its situation at the mouth of the Meon but the Earl constructed a dam across the mouth of the river to irrigate his land and built a canal instead. Titchfield Canal, regarded as one of the oldest artificial waterways in Britain, dates back to the seventeenth century. Originally intended to serve barge traffic between Titchfield and the sea, it was never a great success and later fell into disuse. Our walk follows the canal, picking our way alongside marsh marigolds, oak trees, flowering rushes and pretty watermeadows which are now part of a nature reserve designed to protect large numbers of wildfowl.

WALK 23

TITCHFIELD –
Sea Breezes

N

A27 **FAREHAM**

TITCHFIELD

P

START/ FINISH

Great Posbrook

Little Posbrook

Nature Reserve

1 Mile

1 Kilometre

From The Square in the centre of **Titchfield**, we walk along South Street. Pass the Coach & Horses pub, then turn right into Coach Hill. Walk through a residential area and bear left into Posbrook Lane. Pass a cemetery and a signposted footpath, then turn right at the sign for **Great Posbrook Farm**. Follow the metalled drive between fields, avoid a path on the left and go round a right-hand bend. After several yards, the path runs to the left of a hedge. Skirt the field, with the boundary on our right, and pass a trig point, a surviving relic from the days when the Ordnance Survey used these triangulation pillars to mark an exact height established by surveying instruments. These days the concrete markers are redundant, superseded by advanced satellite technology.

Follow the path round the field corner and keep going to the next corner. Pass through a gap in the trees and follow the path along the edge of some woodland. Turn right at a drive, known as Brownwich Lane, and follow it to the road. Bear left along Common Lane to the junction with Warsash Road. Turn left and walk along to Hunts Pond Road. In order to avoid the traffic, follow the walkway parallel to Warsash Road and then join Hook Lane, signposted Solent Breezes. Follow the road between fields and trees and on reaching a sign on the left for Chilling coastal area, we join a permitted path between fences. The path passes under some pylons and then crosses a track. Continue ahead, skirting a field, with trees and hedgerow on the left.

At the field corner, follow the path into a wood. Go through the trees, then turn left and skirt another field. Turn left at the next main junction, go straight on when the track curves left after about 70 yards, and follow the path to the Solent shore. Wherever we venture in the world, the uniting of land and sea always makes an impression on our senses and our emotions; the Solent waves lapping gently in front of us at this stage of the walk is no exception. Bear left at the beach, cross a wooden footbridge, then take the path the short distance up to the cliff top. Follow the Solent Way towards Titchfield Haven and pass a footpath on the left. This stretch of the long-distance trail offers fine views over Hampshire's coastline. Cross three stiles before reaching a private beach and follow the signposted path behind some chalets to reach the road by a sign for Meon Shore. Cross the road to a path and bear left.

The Solent, looking across to the Isle of Wight

Follow the path as it runs parallel to the road. Avoid a stile on the left, where the road bends left, and continue to the next stile, where there is an information board about the area. Turn right here and head north towards Titchfield, following the path between the old canal and the nature reserve. Pass a bridge and a footpath on the left, cross a stile by the **nature reserve** sign, and continue ahead. We can spot a picturesque thatched cottage on the opposite bank now. Go through a gate and when the track turns left to cross the canal, go straight on through several kissing gates. Cross the road and continue on the path. Cross a footbridge to **Titchfield church** and return to the village centre where the walk began.

Walk 24 – Forest of Bere

Wickham and Soberton Heath

Distance:	4½ miles
Start/Finish:	Station Car Park, Station Close, Wickham
Terrain:	Bridleways and forest tracks; may be muddy!
Parking:	At the start
Maps:	OS Landranger sheet 196
	OS Explorer sheet 119
Refreshments:	Good choice in Wickham town centre
Information:	Meon Valley Railway Walk: 023 9246 2879
	West Walk (Forestry Commission):
	01420 23666

With its medieval market square hemmed in by an engaging collection of small, independent shops, Wickham is one of Hampshire's most attractive little towns. It was the birthplace of William of Wykeham, founder of both Winchester College and New College, Oxford. Although of humble peasant stock, William had led a charmed life. By the time of his appointment as Bishop of Winchester in 1367, he had become a man of considerable wealth; he transformed the interior of his great Norman cathedral, and personally endowed the two prestigious colleges that continue to flourish almost 600 years after his death. Educated in Winchester, William had caught the eye of Bishop Edington, who introduced him to Edward III. In a secular career spanning twenty years, he rose to be Chief Surveyor of the Royal Castles and Warden of Forests and Woods.

It was, perhaps, a fitting appointment. At that time Wickham itself stood close to the centre of the Forest of Bere, a great swathe of woodland stretching from the Sussex border to the River Test. Saxon kings had hunted over this land since long

WALK 24

WICKHAM AND THE FOREST OF BERE

SOBERTON HEATH

Disused Railway

A32

N

P

START/FINISH

Mill

WICKHAM

1 Mile

1 Kilometre

before the Norman Conquest, but it was left to King William to declare Bere a Royal Forest in 1086. Charles I led the last Royal hunt in 1628, by which time the Forest was being stripped of its timber for the nearby naval dockyards.

Our route takes us deep within West Walk, the largest surviving fragment of the former Royal Forest, and a charming mixture of nineteenth-century oak and more modern conifer *plantations. The area is now a Forest Nature Reserve, with a variety of facilities for visitors.*

The small **Station Car Park** on the north-eastern outskirts of Wickham is easy enough to find. But don't expect to see signposts to the railway station – it closed in 1955! Almost half a century later there is little here to interest the railway enthusiast, though the impressive bridges still make useful landmarks on the bridleway which now follows the abandoned line between Wickham and West Meon.

The car park backs directly onto the bridleway and we turn left, heading north *without* crossing the bridge over the River Meon. Follow the old line as far as the first overbridge; a few yards beyond the brick arch, take the path that doubles back to the left and climbs up out of the cutting to the farm track at the top. Turn left again, crossing over the railway and following the track as it winds past the picturesque Northfields Farm and Chiphall Lake to the main A32.

There is no footway here, so take great care as we turn left and follow this busy main road for the next 200 yards. Pass two white-washed lodge cottages on the right-hand side, and head for the wooden gates leading into the safe haven of West Walk, also on the right-hand side. A maze of waymarked trails for walkers, cyclists and horse riders criss-cross these Forestry Commission woodlands, and our own route stitches several of these trails together to form an almost direct north-easterly line through the forest.

Begin by following the red waymarked trail at right angles to the road; then, after just 75 yards, leave the main ride and fork left. Ignore all turnings, and follow the trail as it dips into a small valley and crosses a brook. We climb back out of the valley and, 300 yards beyond the brook, arrive at a five-way junction. Keep straight on here, now following the prominent green waymarks of the Family Cycle Route. Follow them straight over the next forest crossroads and, 250 yards further on, stick with the Cycle Route as it forks left onto a narrow track signposted 'Woodend trail and car park'.

After 300 yards the Cycle Route bears off to the right; keep straight on here, dropping down to cross a gravelled forest ride. Four hundred yards further on keep a sharp eye out for two white horseshoe waymarks, one after the other, on the right of the path. Between them, turn off to the left, pass a red waymark, and immediately cross a small brook at a tiny ford. Now we climb up a short hill and, after 200 yards, emerge from the forest at a gate on the road to **Soberton Heath**.

Turn left, then take the first turning on the right, signposted to Swanmore and Curdridge. Follow the road for 250 yards, as far as a small lay-by on the left-hand side. From here a rather unpromising little track, well-used by horses, drops down towards the **old railway**. We join the old line just south of the road bridge and turn left, for two miles of easy walking back to the **car park**.

Walk 25 – The Itchen Navigation

Winchester to Eastleigh

Distance:	7 miles
Start:	Winchester (King Alfred's statue, Broadway)
Finish:	Eastleigh railway station
Terrain:	Canal towpath – muddy in places
Parking:	Monday to Saturday: Winchester's Park & Ride buses set down at the Guildhall, close to the start; afterwards, ride back to your car from Winchester railway station (01256 464501 for further information)
	Sunday: Chesil Street car park
Maps:	OS Landranger sheet 185
	OS Explorer sheet 132 (except last mile)
Refreshments:	Bridge Hotel, Shawford; garden centre tea shop, Brambridge
Information:	Tourist Information Centre, The Guildhall, Winchester: 01962 840500

Although records suggest that Bishop Godfrey de Lucy first improved the Itchen to carry river traffic during the reign of King John, it wasn't until 1665 that Parliament authorised the Itchen Navigation. The Mayor and citizens of Winchester had petitioned for the new link which, they thought, would benefit trade and employment in the City.

But the undertaking was never really viable and, as it struggled from one crisis to another, no less than five further Acts of Parliament attempted to put things right. Tolls were increased by the final Act of 1820, but soon the Navigation was overtaken by events. In 1831 a prospectus was issued for the London and Southampton Railway; its promoters moved quickly, and opened

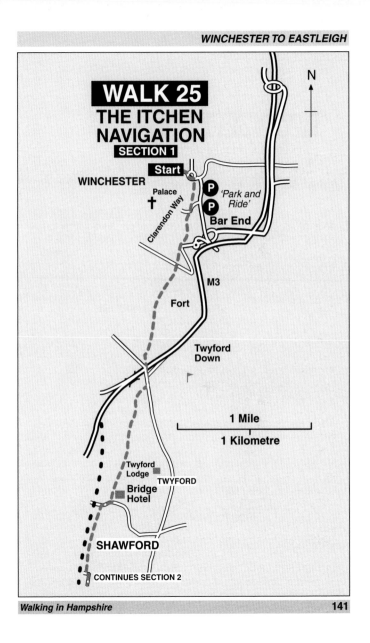

WALK 25
THE ITCHEN
NAVIGATION
SECTION 1

Start

WINCHESTER

Palace
†

'Park and Ride'

Clarendon Way

Bar End

M3

Fort

Twyford
Down

1 Mile

1 Kilometre

Twyford
Lodge

TWYFORD

**Bridge
Hotel**

SHAWFORD

CONTINUES SECTION 2

N

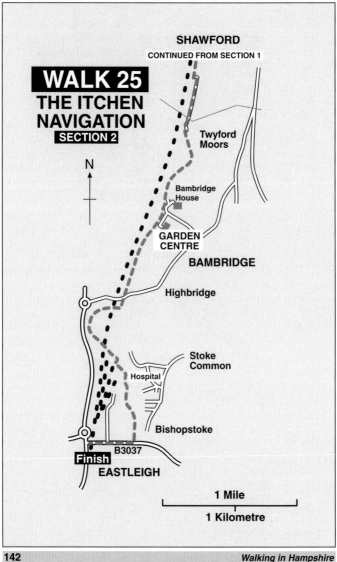

the section of line between Winchester and Southampton in June 1839. Traffic on the waterway, never brisk, just dwindled away and in 1869 Robert Newton piloted his barge up to Winchester with its last load of coal. Soon afterwards, the Company finally closed its books.

Yet water supply and drainage were always a part of the Navigation's function and, consequently, it hasn't slipped into oblivion like grander ventures that relied solely on water-borne traffic. Much of the route still exists to this day, and the section from Winchester to Eastleigh makes a pleasant walk down this attractive valley. Some of the original eleven locks can still be seen along the way, now mostly converted to weirs. On the outskirts of Eastleigh there are glimpses of a more industrial landscape, but this quiet backwater is mainly rural walking.

Start from King Alfred's statue, close by the Guildhall in **Winchester's Broadway**, and walk east down the short High Street. Just before the City Bridge we turn right beside the Old Monk pub, and join the riverside walk beside the fast-flowing River Itchen. After about 300 yards we turn left, and cross the river in front of the imposing brick built Wharf Mill. Now we turn right, and join Wharf Hill for about 100 yards until it swings away to the right. Here we keep straight ahead into an unmade road and, 50 yards further on, a wooden footpath sign points our way down a path to the right. Follow it to Wharf Bridge, and recross the waterway.

This was Blackbridge Wharf, head of the 10½ mile Navigation which linked Winchester to the tidal portion of the Itchen at Woodmill, near Southampton. Although the waterway was authorised in 1665 – and should have been completed by 1671 – construction actually dragged on until about 1710. Parliament had granted the promoters an operating monopoly, but they seem to have had little sense of commercial reality. There were persistent complaints about 'exorbitant rates' and poor service, resulting in several further Acts to widen competition and regulate traffic.

We turn south at Wharf Bridge, keeping the waterway on our left for the short half mile to Tun Bridge. Here we zigzag left and right across the Navigation, and follow the towpath as it squeezes between the canal and the rounded bulk of St Catherine's Hill.

*In the 1930s, the new Winchester bypass was shoe-horned into this narrow gap, already shared by the Navigation, the Didcot to Southampton railway, and the old Twyford road. For all its faults – which are many – the controversial motorway over **Twyford Down** has at least allowed this corridor to be restored as a peaceful haven for wildlife, walkers and cyclists.*

Half a mile further on, just beyond the nature reserve access at Plague Pits valley, look out for the remains of Catherine Hill lock half-hidden in the trees to our right. Soon the path dives under an old brick railway bridge, and comes alongside the M3 motorway on its high embankment to our left; ahead of us, on the right, look out for the disused Shawford railway viaduct. The Navigation has been culverted here, so we follow the tarmac path to the traffic lights and join the signed pedestrian route towards **Twyford**, sharing the road bridge under the motorway.

A hundred yards beyond the bridge sanity is restored as we turn right onto the Itchen Navigation footpath opposite the entrance to Hockley Golf Club. Keep left at the new wooden footbridge, and rejoin the Navigation as it swings in from our right. Soon the path crosses a sluice, and the River Itchen sidles off to the left; our path follows the Navigation, still on the right-hand side. Half a mile – and several stiles – further on, we pass the remains of the shallow Compton Lock. Soon the back gardens rolling down to the far side of the water announce our arrival in **Shawford** village, where the canal-side **Bridge Hotel** makes a comfortable lunch-time stop.

We leave Shawford with the waterway on our left; soon, we join a tarmac lane sandwiched between the Navigation and the railway, but our path cuts away to the left just beyond the next railway arch. Four hundred yards further on we jump the stile by some farm build-ings and zigzag left and right across the bridge, waymarked Itchen Way. The path veers away from the Navigation and picks up a farm track, still signposted as the Itchen Way; we follow it for 400 yards before recrossing the waterway just below the derelict College Mead Lock.

With the waterway once again on our left, we rejoin the towpath for the charming three-quarter mile section to **Brambridge**. Look out for the unique wickerwork fishing lodge on the far bank, and pass the fast flowing section below Brambridge lock where the trout leap out of the water on their way upstream. As we cross the Otterbourne–Brambridge road the towpath changes sides once again and, if you feel peckish, a short walk up the road to the left brings us to Brambridge **garden centre** with its attractive tea shop.

Beyond the road the towpath continues along the narrow bank separating the Navigation on the right, from the river on the left. Soon the river swings away, the railway draws steadily closer across the water to the right and, a mile beyond Brambridge, we come to Allbrook lock.

In fact the railway is so close here that, before it was opened in 1839, the railway company rebuilt the lock with the substantial brick chamber that now houses a 'staircase weir' in place of the original gates. The Navigation, never strongly commercial, survived for a mere thirty years after the railway opened. Traffic had always been predominantly one-way, and towards the end income trickled in from a variety of sources; Winchester College, for instance, paid an annual £20 for scholars' bathing rights!

Beyond the Allbrook road the Navigation swings hard right and dives through a brick arch bridge beneath the railway. Across the water to our right, the light industrial depot soon gives way to houses and gardens fringing the far bank, and watermeadows open up on the left. For half a mile the waterway veers back to the left, until it finally burrows through a low arch under the railway. The path is uneven here, so tread carefully.

Once more east of the line, the extensive railway sidings at **Eastleigh** close in across the water; 200 yards beyond the bridge, the path swings abruptly to the right and crosses the waterway on the site of Withymead lock. With the Navigation now on our left, it's plain sailing to **Bishopstoke** lock, just north of the B3037. Turn right onto the main road for the last half mile to Eastleigh station, and trains back to Winchester.

Walk 26: Kingsley's Walk

Micheldever Wood

Distance:	6½ miles
Start/Finish:	Micheldever Wood
Terrain:	Broad, well-drained tracks with a short section across fields
Parking:	Forestry Commission car park
Map:	OS Landranger sheet 185 OS Explorer sheet 132
Refreshments:	Trout Inn, Itchen Abbas
Information:	Tourist Information Centre, The Guildhall, Winchester: 01962 840500

Across the high chalk downs that guard the valley of the Itchen strides a network of ancient trackways unparalleled in southern England. These old roads were for centuries the area's only transport links, and they still provide the best way of enjoying the countryside in this corner of Hampshire.

During the summer of 1862, Charles Kingsley settled in the Itchen valley to complete the manuscript of The Waterbabies. At first he stayed at Alresford with a Mrs Marx, whom he described as '... one of the most agreeable women I have ever met, but she weighs 16 stones and has a moustache.' Later on, Kingsley moved to The Plough (now the Trout Inn) at Itchen Abbas. Many of Tom's underwater adventures almost certainly took place in the Itchen, where Kingsley made the most of the peace and quiet for a few days fishing. 'Oh, the loveliness of this vale and river!' he wrote in a letter home. 'I am just starting fishing – day looking perfect: but I don't hope for much, the fish are all feeding at ground ...' Indeed the river was the perfect inspiration for this part of the book, and much of his time was spent gazing into streams '... so clear that none could see where water ended and where air began.'

Turn left out of the Forestry Commission car park in **Micheldever Wood** and after about 200 yards fork right down the woodland byway. The path soon leaves the woods, and if we're lucky we may glimpse deer grazing in the fields which border Itchen Wood on our right. The path now bears to the right, and drops gently downhill; at the bottom of the slope turn left onto a broad, grassy track.

A couple of hundred yards further on, a path swings in from the right. This will be our homeward track, but for now keep straight on. After about half a mile, we come to a windpump on our left; just past the pump, fork left onto a gravel track, heading away from the buildings of Itchen Down Farm on our right. This is skylark country, the broad track giving wide views despite the tall hedgebanks on either hand. Crossing the little Itchen Abbas to East Stratton road, we follow the path as it climbs gently between wire fences onto Itchen Stoke Down.

Look to the right as the path levels out, for this is hallowed ground. In the closing years of the eighteenth century, as Europe descended into the mire of the French Wars, the cricketers of Hambledon took on and defeated England's best on Broadhalfpenny, Windmill and Stoke Downs. Their first recorded match against England, here on Stoke Down, was in July 1778; the Hambledon team lost, but the following year England came back to Stoke Down and were beaten in the return match.

Altogether County cricket was played here for nearly thirty years, the Hampshire side beating England on four of their six visits. But this wasn't the game we know today. On a stony patch of cut pasture two, not three, stumps marked each end of the wicket. Players wearing a motley of bright colours bowled underarm to batsmen wielding curved bats and, out on the boundary, the scorers kept tallies on notched sticks.

The five-way junction on Itchen Stoke Down will try to lead us astray. Ignoring the path which trails in from our left, we turn 90 degrees to the right and coast downhill on a pleasant, grassy path between hedges of hawthorn and dog rose. A short mile further on, we cross the silent tracks of the Mid-Hants Railway, bear right, and drop smartly down to the B3047 at **Itchen Abbas**.

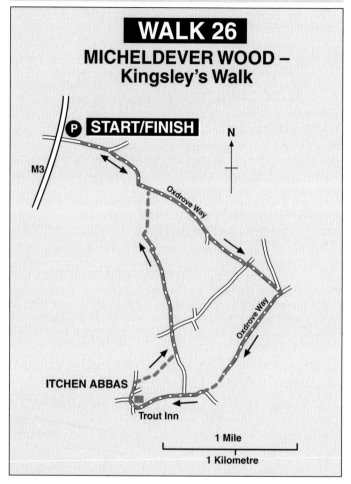

WALK 26
MICHELDEVER WOOD –
Kingsley's Walk

Messrs Smith and Hunt began constructing the Alton, Alresford and Winchester Railway in 1861. On the strength of plans for a branch to Meonstoke, the company changed its name to the Mid-Hants Railway and built all the earthworks and bridges to double track standards. Yet the projected branch remained a dream, and the Mid-Hants opened in 1865 with a single track; it was never doubled.

The line was absorbed into the Southern Railway in 1923 and, in the years that followed, the watercress trade through Alresford reached its peak. But there were cut-backs during the 1930s and, later on, the line was left out of the Southern's electrification programme.

The closure notices posted in 1967 met intense opposition, and objectors forced two public inquiries in a spirited defence that lasted six years. It was not quite in vain. Although the last British Railways train ran over the Mid-Hants in February 1973, the Alton–Alresford section survived into preservation, and is now a tourist attraction with a history of its own.

To begin with, this section of roadway has no pavement, so we must take care as we turn right for the last half mile into the village, where the **Trout Inn** makes a good lunchtime stop.

After lunch we turn right out of the Trout, then right again after a hundred yards, up the back road signposted 'School'. Soon we pass under a bridge carrying the old railway high overhead, and turn immediately right by the little wooden footpath sign, into a farmyard. Keeping the wooden farm buildings on our left, we pass through the five-bar gate and over the stile just beyond it. Continue climbing slowly, and cross another stile a hundred yards further on. Now turn 45 degrees left, and cross two fields on the same heading. There is a stile between these fields, and another which brings us out onto a minor road.

Turn left up this little lane and, after about a quarter of a mile, go straight over the crossroads onto a gravel track. The track climbs steadily for about half a mile, and we'll make a point of stopping on this section to look at the unrivalled views across the Itchen valley behind us. The lane now takes a couple of right and left double bends, before falling gently between wire fences to rejoin our outward route about a third of a mile further on. Turn left, and then right after a couple of hundred yards; finally retrace the last half mile to our starting point in the **car park**.

Walk 27 – On the Dole

New Alresford

Distance:	8 miles
Start/Finish:	New Alresford town centre
Terrain:	Mostly well-defined farm tracks once clear of the town; however, some sections using field paths may be muddy
Parking:	Pay and display car park at the railway station
Map:	OS Landranger sheet 185 OS Explorer sheet 132
Refreshments:	The Cricketers, Tichborne Down; the Flower Pots Inn, Cheriton; the Tichborne Arms, Tichborne
	Wide choice in Alresford town centre
Information:	Tourist Information Centre, The Guildhall, Winchester: 01962 840500

Our walk begins in New Alresford, founded by Bishop Godfrey de Lucy towards the end of the twelfth century. The holy man enclosed Alresford Pond behind the Great Weir, and records suggest that he improved the Itchen to carry river traffic at his own expense. A disastrous series of fires in the fifteenth, seventeenth and eighteenth centuries destroyed most of Alresford's original timber-framed buildings and, as a result, the town boasts a good deal of elegant Georgian architecture.

In the years before the Second World War, the town became the focus for the local watercress trade, with daily loads of 8 or 9 tons being despatched by train via the Mid-Hants Railway. But the 'Watercress Line' fell victim to British Railways' rationalisation plans and, despite a six-year battle by local residents, the Alton–Winchester section was closed in 1973. By then, the preservation

WALK 27
NEW ALRESFORD –
On The Dole

N

START/FINISH

NEW ALRESFORD

P

Cricketers

A31

Vernal
Farm

Wayferer's Walk

TICHBORNE

Tichborne
Arms

CHERITON

Flower
Pots Inn

1 Mile

1 Kilometre

movement was gearing itself up to save the line as far as Alresford, and the railway is now a major tourist attraction.

For the first mile we follow the waymarked **Wayfarer's Walk**, joining the trail as it noses into St John's churchyard beside Barclays Bank. Keep the church on the left, and follow the tarmac path as it zigzags through the churchyard. At the railway cutting the path swings left beside the railway, emerging onto Sun Hill where we turn right across the railway bridge.

Pass the school on the right, and drop down the hill towards the bypass. At the foot of the hill follow the road round to the right, past Sun Cottage; after about 150 yards, follow the Wayfarer's Walk as it turns left, up and over the bypass footbridge. On the far side of the bridge we leave the Wayfarer's Walk, following the bridleway to the left, signposted towards Bramdean.

After a further 150 yards, turn right through a wicket gate leading onto Alresford golf course, signposted 'Bridleway'. The well-defined track is sheltered by stands of oak and beech as it crosses the golf course – but we'll keep an eye out for flying golf balls just the same! At the end of this section we climb gently through a delightful tree-shaded tunnel, along the edge of an old hazel coppice. At the top of the woods the path levels off momentarily, and zigzags left and right near the water treatment works.

The pleasant old lane now climbs once again between hedgerow trees. A quarter of a mile further on, the lane from Scrubb Farm swings in from the left; but our way continues confidently up the slight rise, always in the company of open fields broken with coppice and light woodland. Pass the radio mast on the brow of the hill, before dropping down into a wide valley. Here we briefly join the lane from Ropley Dean to Cheriton as it zigzags across our path, before continuing straight ahead along a green lane waymarked Wayfarer's Walk Circular Route *(WWCR)*.

The small-scale woods and coppice which have kept us company from the golf course have fallen behind now, and we embark upon a more open, arable landscape, walking between low hedges. Pass under the power lines, and up to the crest of small rise.

The fields on our right are peaceful now, but, on 29 March 1644,

Lawrence Oxley's famous bookshop in New Alresford

this was the scene of one of the pivotal battles of the English Civil War. More than two thousand men died in the space of three hours as Sir William Waller's Parliamentarian battalions massacred the Royalist forces under Lord Hopton's command.

We drop down the slight slope from the battlefield until Cheriton Wood nuzzles the path on our left and, at the end of the wood, follow the *WWCR* along the footpath to the right. After half a mile we come to a small gate, cross a green lane, and keep straight along Upper

Lamborough Lane. The large arable fields are scattered with trees, and even a line of small electricity pylons does little to spoil the views across this broad green valley.

After a quarter of a mile a green lane crosses our route; nip over the stile opposite and take the field-edge path, still waymarked *WWCR*. Follow the waymarking along the field-edge path until at length the path dives between hedges and drops down into **Cheriton**, narrowing all the time. Eventually the hedges are replaced by wooden fences, and a small step-stile leads us out onto a gravelled access road. Turn right as far as Freeman's Yard, cross the stream by the bridge, and follow the village road round to the left and onto the green by the Post Office Stores.

Fancy a beer? If so, we can turn left at the War Memorial, then immediately right, signposted Winchester (A272). The **Flower Pots Inn**, which is a free house, is about 200 yards up this road on the left.

Otherwise turn right at the war memorial and, after 200 yards, swing left up the lane to Hill Houses. The banks of this sunken lane are draped with ivy, old man's beard and hart's tongue fern. At Colcut Cottage we follow the obvious road, bearing to the right onto an attractive green lane overhung with yew, holly, beech and oak. Our way is soon joined by a lane from the left, and we climb out of the sunken hollow onto a fairly level plateau with green fields, trees and hedges on either hand.

The lane winds on for half a mile until we come to a line of electricity pylons. Directly underneath them, dive off to the right along the narrow path through a finger of woodland extending northwards towards Tichborne. On the far side of the woods a small wooden gate leads out into an area of large open fields. Follow the field boundary on the right until it swings sharply to the right; then bear just slightly to the right for about 200 yards, heading for the 'Off-road cycle trail' waymark at the corner of the hedge on the far side of the field. Here we turn right, keeping the hedge on our left, and steering towards a large black corrugated iron barn. The tower of Tichborne church is visible to the right of this barn in the middle distance, just beyond the corner of Fulley Wood.

Still keeping the hedge on our left we pass through a metal farm gate, and join the gently sloping track that follows the valley down towards Tichborne; Alresford is just visible in the far distance.

The lane joins the village road at Grange Farm, and we turn left towards **Tichborne** itself. Follow the road as it winds through the village, past the **Tichborne Arms**, as good a place as any to mug up on a little local history.

In the tenth century, 'Ticceburn' formed part of the Bishop of Winchester's estate, which at that time included the modern parishes of Cheriton and Beauworth. The Saxon farmers paid tithes of beer, ale, bread and cheese, together with sheep, oxen and pigs – or fish, if the payment fell due in Lent!

The Bishop granted part of this huge estate to Walter de Tichborne around the year 1135, and his descendants have lived here ever since. The family held to the Catholic faith at the Reformation, and the Anglican church of St Andrew, just up the lane opposite the pub, is almost unique in having a Catholic chapel in the north aisle.

The Tichborne Dole is one of the oldest traditions in Britain, dating back to the twelfth or thirteenth century. In honour of Lady Mabella Tichborne's dying wish for bread to be distributed to the poor, a measure of flour is still 'doled out' to the parishioners each Lady Day. But the Lady's wish was subject to the oddest condition; her husband agreed to dedicate all the corn from the land she could crawl around while a torch was burning. The spirited lady managed a circuit of 23 acres, and to this day these same fields are known as 'The Crawls'.

Walk right through the village, and at length turn right onto the bridleway at **Vernal Farm**, where a wooden finger post and Itchen Way marker confirm our route. Once past the farm buildings, the lane becomes a pleasant grassy track with hedges on each side; the bypass sweeps across the valley to the left, and New Alresford is now firmly in our sights.

Soon the lane bends, still waymarked Itchen Way, and follows the top of the bypass cutting. In a quarter of a mile we rise up to the B3046, turn left across the bridge, and immediately right into Tichborne Down at the **Cricketers** pub. After half a mile the road swings left into Sun Hill, and we retrace our outward steps back to the town centre.

Walk 28: Along the Itchen Valley

North of Winchester

Distance:	8 miles
Start/Finish:	Winchester Cathedral
Terrain:	Mainly riverside paths; will be muddy after rain
Parking:	Monday to Saturday: Winchester Park & Ride (01256 464501 for more information) Sunday: Chesil Street car park
Maps:	OS Landranger sheet 185 OS Explorer sheet 132
Refreshments:	Cart and Horses, Kings Worthy Cricketers or Chestnut Horse, Easton Extensive choice in city centre
Information:	Tourist Information Centre, The Guildhall, Winchester: 01962 840500

Our walk begins at the great west door of Winchester Cathedral, and tiptoes out of town between nature reserve and trading estate. Yet it soon shakes itself clear of England's ancient capital and takes on a largely rural character. The rich wildlife of the Itchen valley is of national importance, and we pass several areas designated as Sites of Special Scientific Interest. The route is dotted with orchids and marsh valerian, knapweed and yellow flag; birdwatchers may spot yellow wagtail, warblers and buntings, as well as pochard, snipe or lapwing.

Facing the **Cathedral**'s west front, we set off through the tiny arch at the right-hand side, following the green and white metal signposts which will guide us as far as Wolvesey Castle. The archway leads under vaulted buttresses down the south side of the Cathedral, and after a few yards the Close opens up to the right. Turn here, and head

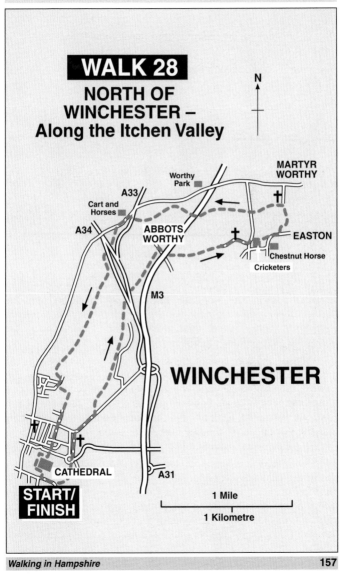

WALK 28

NORTH OF WINCHESTER – Along the Itchen Valley

N

MARTYR WORTHY

Worthy Park

A33

Cart and Horses

A34

ABBOTS WORTHY

EASTON

Chestnut Horse

Cricketers

M3

WINCHESTER

CATHEDRAL

A31

START/ FINISH

1 Mile

1 Kilometre

The Kingsgate arch, Winchester

diagonally across the Close to the half timbered Porters Lodge on the far side. Turning right again, go through the arched gateway that leads out into St Swithun Street; then, almost at once, turn left under the Kingsgate arch and left into College Street.

Walk all the way down College Street, passing the 600-year old College on the right. After 400 yards look out for Wolvesey Castle on the left and, as College Walk swings off to the right, keep straight on down the broad tarmac path signposted 'High St via steps'. From here, it's a pleasant 400 yard stroll between the medieval City walls and the River Itchen to the City Bridge.

Climb the few steps onto the bridge, cross the road, and turn right over the bridge; in a few yards, just before The Cricketers, slip away to the left down Water Lane. Follow the road for some 300 yards beside the river, until Durngate Bridge swings in from the left; then keep straight on into Wales Street, passing both the Ship Inn and the First In – Last Out. Soon we come to a small industrial estate on our left-hand side; cross over Nickel Close, and almost at once turn left up a small un-named road. Walk past the brick built bungalows on the right, and after about 100 yards cross over a stile into the field straight ahead. There are generally cows here, so it can be muddy.

To begin with the field is quite narrow, with a steep bank on the right; but soon the bank drops away, and we pass through a gate into the next field. Across the trees to the right are the warehouses of the Winnall trading estate, but go quietly along the left-hand edge of the field, and you may catch a glimpse of wildfowl on the lakes beyond the hedgerow. At length the field narrows away to nothing, and ends at a stile. Jump over here, and follow the pathway straight ahead.

In a short way there is a slight kink in the path, which is now bounded by a post and wire fence to the left, and the low bank of the old Southampton to Didcot railway on the right. Nowadays, the old line forms the trading estate boundary, but the path shrugs it off as it runs through a tunnel of overgrown hedges.

Suddenly on the left, a view opens up across the wide reed beds of the reserve to the houses of Headbourne Worthy on the hill beyond. Here you may catch a glimpse of the striking reed bunting, or of the reed and sedge warblers that fly in for the summer. The birds seem oblivious to the noise of the A34, which has been drawing ever closer on our right. All at once, the path meets the River Itchen and turns sharp right under the road, which is carried on two bridges in quick succession.

Mind your head at the second bridge, where the concrete girders sweep low over the steel walkway that carries the path. Once under the bridges, the path zigzags hard right, then left, briefly skirting the edge of an open field on the right. As the river bears off to the left and the noise of the road dies away, the path widens into a pleasant grassy track. In late summer the chalk bank to the right is ablaze with knapweed; on the left, the hedgerow trees are clothed in glossy dark green ivy.

Soon a field opens up to the right, bounded on the far side by the embankment of the M3 motorway. The tall hedgerow trees continue along the left-hand side of this field; follow them as far as the low brick buildings beside the tennis court on the right. Here the path meets a tarmac drive known as the Long Walk; we turn right, and soon dive under the M3 bridge.

Just here, turn left up the grassy track signposted 'right of way'; don't be misled down the pumping station access road, which runs immediately to the left of this track. Half a mile's pleasant walking brings us to **Easton**, and there are fine views of **Worthy Park** beyond the M3 to our left.

Worthy Park came into the Ogle family in the mid eighteenth century, and the present house was built by Sir Charles Ogle in 1820. Charles pursued a successful naval career and, although his ship was laid up for repairs during the Battle of Trafalgar, he was ultimately appointed Admiral of the Fleet in 1857. But wealth and power were no protection against personal tragedy; his first wife had died in 1814, and his only child by his second wife Letitia was born a total invalid. In 1825 the family sold the estate to Samuel Wall, whose descendants lived there until the house was requisitioned during the Second World War.

The track enters the village at the white-painted Malms Cottage; just beyond it on the left is the much larger Old Rectory. Follow the lane down past the twelfth-century St Mary's church, to the small green at the junction near the **Cricketers** pub. Turn left, and after 100 yards look out for a stile and a wooden footpath sign on the right, opposite Market Garden cottage. Jump the stile, and head for the far right-hand corner of the field. Here a second stile leads into a narrow fenced path, which soon emerges onto the village road beside the **Chestnut Horse** pub. Turn left, and follow the road for 100 yards beyond the right-hand bend; here, a metal public footpath sign points our way left, up the drive to Flint Cottage and Paidon.

Turn left up this gravelled track, and pass through a small metal gate at the top; turn right here, then in 50 yards left again. Follow the barbed-wire fence on the left, and cross the gated footbridge over the stream. A little further on, a larger wooden bridge carries us over the main river to the foot of the small lane leading up into **Martyr Worthy** village. A short way up this lane, just past the half-timbered Tumbledown, follow the wooden footpath sign which points left up a few steps onto a narrow path between the gardens. The path swings left and right, crosses a stile, then leads us back beside the river to Easton Bridge.

Cross over the road here and jump the stile straight ahead,

St Andrew's church is unusual for the Catholic chapel it houses (Walk 27)

Looking towards King's Somborne (Walk 31)

following the wooden footpath sign along the edge of a grassy field. At first, the fence is on our right; after 200 yards, we cross another stile to put it on our left. Keep straight ahead beside this fence as far as the M3 embankment; then nip over the stile on the left and follow the path, under the motorway, to a second stile.

From here, our way runs up the left-hand edge of the field ahead, with Worthy Park across the Itchen Abbas road to our right. Soon we join this road via another stile, turning left past the twin gateways leading to The Worthys, and tackle a further stile on the left. A little wooden footpath sign points diagonally across the next field, past the left-hand corner of a low wooden barn, to an iron kissing gate in the far corner.

Go through the gate, cross Mill Lane, and join the narrow path straight ahead. After the first 100 yards it zigzags right and left over a ditch, and opens into a short informal avenue lined with holly, yew and beech. Soon we approach the A33, and fork right up the bank before crossing over the busy dual carriageway. Keep straight on up the grassy track marked by a wooden footpath sign, emerging after 100 yards directly opposite the **Cart and Horses** pub. Turn left here, and follow the London Road towards Winchester.

Much of the next section was described by author Hilaire Belloc in his book The Old Road, *published in 1904. Belloc wanted to establish the exact route of the old Pilgrims' Way from Winchester to Canterbury and, after presenting his case, he set out to walk the track himself: 'We left Hyde Street by the first opening in the houses of its eastern side; we halted with regret at the stable door ... which is the last relic of Hyde Abbey. We saw the little red-brick villas, new built and building, that guard the grave where Alfred lay in majesty for six hundred years.' A century later, his old road still carries the occasional pilgrim bound for Canterbury on foot.*

After 200 yards turn left through the lychgate, pass through St Mary's churchyard, then bear right along the edge of the playing field. At the end of the trees keep straight ahead in front of Peek's offices as far as the A34 embankment. Here, a small wooden footpath sign points our way left down a narrow path, keeping the road on our right. In less than 100 yards the path swings to the right, and burrows through two bridges under the road.

The Cathedral Church of St Swithun's, consecrated in 1093

Notice the old brick arch sandwiched between the newer concrete structures of the first bridge. The original arch carried the old Great Western Railway line to Newbury; it lies just south of the site of Kings Worthy station, now lost forever under modern tarmac.

After the second bridge the path swings back to the left and follows the foot of the embankment as far as the River Itchen, where it turns abruptly to the right through a gap in the fence. Shortly the path zigzags over a white railed footbridge, and we embark on a pleasant stroll through open country, with a small brook for company on our left.

Half a mile further on we cross over the concrete bridge at Chalkdell Cottage, and carry on down the gravelled road, now with the stream on our right. Soon the road swings off to the right over another bridge, but our way lies straight ahead down the gravelled footpath beside the stream. A little further on the path is crossed by Hillier Way, running down from the Abbots Barton estate on the far side of the brook. Looking back from here across the small green, we can glimpse the tall brick chimneys of the picturesque Tudor farm-house at Abbots Barton.

Now we are on the outskirts of **Winchester**, with tarmac under-foot. Keep straight on as far as the allotment gardens across the stream, where a grassy bank opens up on the left-hand side just before the row of red-brick houses backing on from Nuns Road. Turn up onto the bank, keeping the football pitch on the left and the houses on the right, and after 100 yards turn right onto the metalled track skirting the edge of the North Walls Recreation Ground.

Follow this track for 50 yards before turning left onto the City Centre cycle way that crosses the playing fields beside a neat line of dark green hornbeams. Cross the white-railed concrete bridge and turn right, keeping the river on the right. Carry on for 200 yards, cross the flint-walled bridge, and pass out through the gate into Park Avenue.

A short way further on we cross over North Walls, keeping straight on into Middle Brook Street; cross Friarsgate and carry on again, keeping the Brooks shopping complex on the right. In little more than a hundred yards we reach Debenhams store and turn right up High Street for a few yards, then left under the arches of St Maurice Covert. Cross Market Lane, and follow the path across the green to the west door of the **Cathedral**.

Walk 29 – Waller's Walk

Kings Worthy

Distance:	6 miles
Start/Finish:	The King Charles, Kings Worthy
Terrain:	Farm tracks and muddy field edge paths
Parking:	Pub car park (patrons only)
Maps:	OS Landranger sheet 185
	OS Explorer sheet 132
Refreshments:	The King Charles at start/finish: none on route
Information:	Tourist Information Centre, The Guildhall, Winchester: 01962 840500

This walk takes in part of the high downland forming the water-shed of the Itchen and Dever valleys, and there are some unsign-posted sections across farmland. The route passes through Waller's Ash, said to be named after Sir William Waller, a Parliamentary general in the English Civil War. Certainly there was a skirmish near here in the October of 1645, and weapons from that period were found almost two hundred years later, whilst digging the great chalk cuttings for the nearby London and Southampton railway.

Head north up the Stoke Charity road from the **King Charles** pub, and swing hard left over the main railway line after 450 yards. A hundred yards further on fork left down the 'no through road' sign-posted to Kingsworthy Kennels. Follow this lane past the kennels to the foot of the hill, carrying on past the unmade turning on the left. In less than 100 yards, as the lane climbs up towards the bridge, slip away to the right through a small opening in the hedge.

Notice the metal fence-posts here, with their curious 'top-hat' section; they're made from rails designed by Isambard Kingdom Brunel for the Great Western Railway's seven-foot gauge lines in the

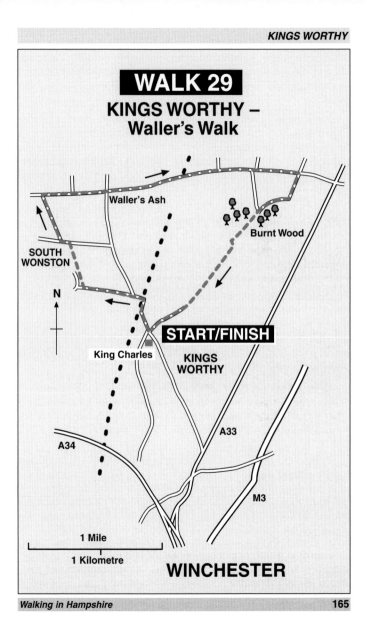

WALK 29
KINGS WORTHY – Waller's Walk

Waller's Ash

Burnt Wood

SOUTH
WONSTON

N

START/FINISH

King Charles

KINGS
WORTHY

A33

A34

M3

1 Mile

1 Kilometre

WINCHESTER

West of England. The last 213 miles of Brunel's broad gauge track were converted to standard gauge during a single weekend in 1892, and the Company used the old rails extensively for fencing and similar jobs.

From the old gateway, a path leads us down to the derelict Worthy Down Halt, on the disused Great Western line from Didcot to Southampton. Bear gently right through the station, and follow the old railway track north. Although the line isn't strictly a right of way, it has been used by walkers and cyclists for many years, and we shouldn't encounter any problems.

After a third of a mile the track is blocked by a bank which carries the Ox Drove east-west across the old railway. Climb up onto the Drove, and turn left towards **South Wonston**. After 150 yards turn up the lane on the right, and at the top of the lane turn right again, onto Alresford Drove. The drove road is usually quiet, but do watch out for the occasional car.

Follow the drove for half a mile, until it crosses Stoke Charity Road by the lonely thatched cottage at **Waller's Ash**, and cross straight over onto the gravelled section for nearly two miles of fast, easy walking. Some way along this stretch we cross over the northern portal of Waller's Ash tunnel, and there are wide views across high downland to the northern horizon.

Now the track swings gently to the right and dips downhill; we enter an avenue of lime trees growing up in the hedge on either hand, and carry on for another 400 yards to the foot of the slope. Here we turn off to the right, down a farm track bordered on the left by a belt of trees.

Follow the track as it drops slightly down and veers hard right towards **Burnt Wood**. Pass through the wood, staying with the track as it curves gently back to the left. As we leave the wood the trees roll back on both sides, opening up a triangular field to our right. Almost at once, a second field opens up on the left; our way lies along the grassy track straight ahead, between these two fields. Follow this track for 200 yards, until it passes through a gap in the hedge straight ahead; then turn right, following the field edge, with the hedge on the right-hand side. At the top corner of the field, as the hedge bends left, pass through the gap and into another field. Turn

The King Charles pub in Kings Worthy marks the end of the walk

left here, along the field edge, this time with the hedge on the left. Stay in this field, turning right at the bottom corner, with the hedge and a small belt of trees still on the left-hand side.

Towards the corner of this field, the hedge is replaced by a barbed-wire fence. Look out for the stile in this fence, and nip over into the adjoining field. Carry on in the same direction for just a few more yards, and cross the next stile as well; with the hedge now on the left, join the muddy farm track that runs between Down Farm and Southstoke Farm. At the farms the track becomes a concrete road which, after a third of a mile, leads us back to our starting point at the **King Charles** pub.

Walk 30 – Sauntering Around Sparsholt

Sparsholt and Farley Mount Country Park

Distance:	5 miles
Start/Finish:	Farley Mount Country Park (Junction car park)
Terrain:	Bridleways and village roads
Parking:	At the start
Map:	OS Landranger sheet 185
	OS Explorer sheet 132
Refreshments:	Plough Inn, Sparsholt
Information:	Tourist Information Centre, The Guildhall, Winchester: 01962 840500

This route encircles the Farley Mount Country Park, over a thousand acres of ancient woods and downland owned by Hampshire County Council. We tread a short section of the old Winchester to Salisbury Roman road, and pass close to the site of Sparsholt Roman villa, excavated in the late 1960s by local archaeologist David Johnston.

Near the start, a curious 30ft high pyramid on Farley Mount marks the burial place of a horse which, in September 1733, 'leaped into a chalk pit twenty-five feet deep a foxhunting with his master on his back'. Horse and owner survived the experience, however, for the following year they won the Hunter's Plate – in the name of 'Beware chalk pit'!

The Junction car park overlooks a wonderful area of open grassland that rolls gently down to the old Roman road bordering West Wood. In good weather it's alive with dog walkers, picnickers and people flying kites.

A few yards west of the **car park** we stroll gently downhill, following the blue-topped waymarks of the bridleway and off-road

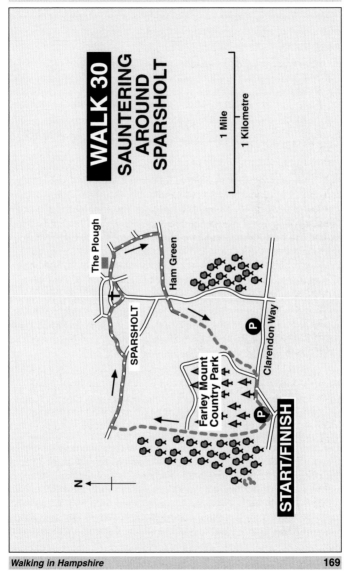

WALK 30

SAUNTERING
AROUND
SPARSHOLT

1 Mile

1 Kilometre

The Plough

Ham Green

SPARSHOLT

Clarendon Way

Farley Mount
Country Park

N

START/FINISH

cycle trail, and skirting the left-hand side of the grassland. At the foot of the hill our way bears slightly to the right, and dives into the woods along a roughly surfaced forest ride.

After half a mile of easy walking, a wedge of farmland drives deep into the forest from the north; we pass through a wooden gate and, as the woods roll back to the right, we follow the left-hand edge of the forest for 100 yards. Now the woods fall away on the left as well. Our way lies straight ahead along a narrow path across the fields, heading for the left-hand end of Ower Wood, the prominent belt of trees on the skyline.

At the far side of the field a wooden bridleway sign and cycle trail waymarks confirm that we've followed the correct path. Dodge through the gap in the wire fence and swing right here, following the farm road through a wide arable landscape. The road leads us through New Barn farmyard, where the road forks; keep left here, and wind up the hill past Moor Court to a T junction at Thatched House. Turn right, and bear right again at the junction with Home Lane, drifting down past the White House as far as St Stephen's church, **Sparsholt**.

The church, which dominates this corner of the village on a brick and flint retaining wall, was founded in the twelfth century. The south aisle was added in the thirteenth century, but another six hundred years elapsed before the north aisle was added during William Butterfield's restoration of 1882. The attractive Burne-Jones window in the south aisle was installed at about the same time.

We turn left at the church, walking past the Memorial Hall and Post Office Stores, before bearing right at the Sparsholt Manor cross-roads. Fifty yards further, on the left, the **Plough Inn** with its garden makes an inviting refreshment stop.

A couple of hundred yards beyond the pub we turn right into Dean Lane, and drop down the hill to the enchanting little hamlet of Dean. Just past Dean Hill Cottage the road swings left at the foot of the hill, but our way lies up the bridleway straight ahead, leaving Barn Cottage on the left. It's muddy at first, but soon the sunken lane climbs steadily away between banks clothed with hazel, yew and holly. After 300 yards a three-way signpost points to the first of two parallel paths across Ham Green Common. Thirty yards further on, turn right at the wooden 'right of way' signpost.

This is **Ham Green Common**, once part of the drovers' road from Salisbury to Winchester, and drovers would camp here overnight with their animals before the last short leg into Winchester market. This track is easier to follow than the path which we passed a little way back, though the lower route may sometimes be less muddy, and offers better views of Sparsholt village on the right-hand side.

After half a mile we cross the Sparsholt road and go straight across onto Burrow Road. This unmade track winds briefly between a couple of bungalows and a barn on the right, before settling into its stride. At first there are tall hedges on each side of the track, but in little more than a quarter of a mile they blend imperceptibly into the woodland. Here our way forms the boundary between Crab Wood on the left and West Wood on the right. The track is crossed and joined by others as we press on through the woods, following the obvious way ahead as far as the green-painted single-bar gate that marks our arrival at the old Sarum Road.

Now we turn right, following the steps of the Legions along the old Roman road from Winchester to Salisbury. A hundred yards further on, the metalled road swings away to the left; we continue straight on, through the small Clarendon car park, following the waymarks of the **Clarendon Way**. This is an area of mixed woodland, with silver birch, hazel, yew and beech now clothing the bank of the Roman road. But a couple of hundred yards brings us back out into the sunshine, on the edge of the open grassland where our walk began. Bear half-left, and stroll up the hillside to the **Junction car park**.

Walk 31 – Ghost Trains and German Bombers

Horsebridge and King's Somborne

Distance:	6 miles
Start/Finish:	Horsebridge, near King's Somborne
Terrain:	Field paths, minor roads and disused railway track
Parking:	Free car park at Horsebridge
Map:	OS Landranger sheet 185 OS Explorer sheet 131
Refreshments:	The John of Gaunt inn, Horsebridge The Crown inn, King's Somborne
Information:	Andover Tourist Information Centre: 01264 324320 Tourism Officer, Test Valley Borough Council: 01264 368836

Lovely chalk downland and fine valley views await us on this varied walk. We start at Horsebridge, a beautifully restored railway station, now run as a restaurant and holiday home. The station, which includes a restored railway carriage and surviving signal box, evokes memories of the golden age of railway travel when remote stations and secluded halts were lovingly cared for by station masters and the sound of an approaching steam train could be heard drifting across the lush countryside. The line, known as the Sprat and Winkle railway, originally ran between Southampton and Cheltenham, and played a key role in both World Wars when it carried troops and supplies to Southampton Docks. There are further reminders of Britain's wartime past as we approach King's Somborne on the Clarendon Way. Here, a memorial stone, half hidden in the hedge, recalls the dark days of 1940 when Britain

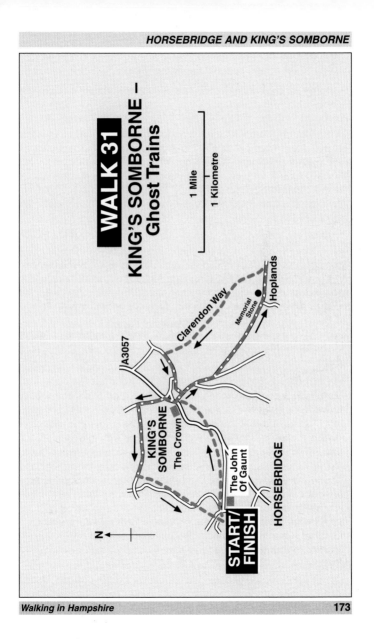

WALK 31

KING'S SOMBORNE –
Ghost Trains

1 Mile
1 Kilometre

Clarendon Way

A3057

Hoplands

Memorial Stone

KING'S SOMBORNE

The Crown

The John Of Gaunt

HORSEBRIDGE

N

START/
FINISH

braced itself for enemy invasion. A German bomber was shot down close to the village, with the loss of four lives.

From the car park we walk towards the **John of Gaunt** inn, bearing right in front of it, then left. *John of Gaunt, son of Edward III, had a deer park close to this spot. Some sources indicate he also built a palace on the banks of the Test though this has been disputed. Excavations carried out in the 1980s produced clues suggesting an Anglo-Saxon settlement but nothing more.* Look for a stile on the left after a few yards and join a path running along the right-hand side of the field. Pass through several wrought-iron kissing gates and go over a ladder-stile, then negotiate a variety of rudimentary gates and stiles before reaching a field.

Head straight across it, keeping to the right of a cream-coloured house, and exit via a gate to the road. Cross over by the 30 mile speed limit sign and take the path up the bank, following it between fences. At the next road turn right, then veer left at the bend. Make for the sports ground and keep to its right-hand boundary. Head for the swings and slides in the corner and negotiate a kissing gate. Follow the path towards the church, keeping to the right of it to reach Church Road. We are now in the centre of **King's Somborne**, one of Hampshire's prettiest villages.

Bear right and pass a turning for Winchester on the left. Continue into Furzedown Road, disregarding Eldon Road on the right. Our surroundings become more rural as we start to leave the village behind us and head into the depths of the countryside. The road climbs steadily and at the top of the slope there are glorious views over open country. Pass the speed derestriction sign and then branch off to the left at the next junction. A welcome seat enables us to pause for a few moments and absorb the view. Follow the minor lane and after nearly a mile we come to **Hoplands**, a small rural settlement consisting of a farm, several houses and an equestrian centre. Once clear of the buildings, we follow a rough track heading east. Pass a sign for Clarendon House and continue along the track, looking for a **memorial stone** in the left-hand hedgerow. The inscription reads: 'In memory of 4 unknown German airmen killed here – August 23rd 1940'.

The air campaign over southern England at the beginning of the

Horsebridge station

Second World War was one of the most crucial and decisive military engagements in history. Incredibly, the sleepy village of King's Somborne was inextricably drawn into the battle for freedom when fighter pilot Bob Doe spotted a lone Junkers 88 bomber in the clouds above the village. Doe launched a deadly attack on the enemy plane and watched as, fatally wounded, it dropped from the skies, spiralling down towards the green fields of Hampshire like a paper dart. Later, he and his squadron leader drove to the spot where the aircraft eventually crashed – a field near King's Somborne. On arrival, they found the wreckage surrounded by Local Defence Volunteers who were there to keep out souvenir hunters and excited villagers. The events of that summer's day more than 60 years ago are not widely recorded. However, the older residents of the area still recall what happened, and the simple memorial stone acts as a permanent reminder to us all.

Keep on the track for a short distance and now we bear sharp left to join the route of the **Clarendon Way**. Follow the path through the wood to a stile, bearing right by some paddocks. Eventually we reach the field corner where there are two stiles; one, ingeniously, has been constructed using the remains of two tree trunks. Continue on the Clarendon Way as it skirts a field and then passes alongside a hedgerow and a line of trees. Below us in the valley, embraced by protective hills, is the village of King's Somborne which we are about to visit once again. Curve to the right and follow the path down to the road.

Turn left and walk along to the centre of the village, passing the old Methodist church on the right, dated 1826. The more modern church stands a little further on along the street, opposite the site of the Andover Arms, now sadly no more. This village hostelry, a perfect example of a traditional, rustic, old-style inn, has made way for a group of modern houses. Pass the King's Somborne working men's club, presented to the working men of the village by George Hennessy, High Sheriff of the county in 1911-12, and head for the junction, turning right towards the **Crown**.

Bear right and walk along Romsey Road, veering left for Cowdrove Hill. Cattle drovers once used this route – hence the name. Further up, by several bungalows, turn left and follow the Clarendon Way parallel to the road. We can pause along here to look back towards King's Somborne, the village nestling snugly below us. The outward leg of the walk can also be traced beyond the jumble of rooftops. Turn left at the next junction and follow the lane to a right-hand bend. Go straight on here and pass the drive to a house on the right. Further down the track we reach the meeting point of the Clarendon Way and the Test Way.

Turn left here and follow the disused trackbed. The glorious Test, which meanders delightfully to our right, is one of Britain's most famous trout and salmon rivers, its valley providing a valuable habitat for birds and other wildlife. Pass the site of John of Gaunt's deer park, as is depicted on the map, cross over one of the many streams and watercourses running through the valley, and eventually we come to a road. Once over it, we continue briefly on the Test Way, passing over another tributary of the river before reaching the old station at **Horsebridge** where our walk began.

Walk 32 – A Hurricane Walk

South-East from Winchester

Distance:	**10 miles**
Start/Finish:	**Winchester (King Alfred's statue, Broadway)**
Terrain:	**Mainly bridleways and green lanes**
Parking:	**Monday to Saturday: Winchester Park & Ride (01256 464501 for more information)** **Sunday: Chesil Street car park**
Map:	**OS Landranger sheet 185** **OS Explorer sheet 132**
Refreshments:	**Shearer's Arms or Ship Inn, Owslebury**
Information:	**Tourist Information Centre, The Guildhall, Winchester: 01962 840500**

'In Hertford, Hereford and Hampshire, hurricanes hardly happen.' The well-known line from My Fair Lady *may have been true once, but the great storm of 1987 brought devastation to many of the woodlands around Winchester. The narrow shelter belts along the Morestead road were particularly badly hit, and it took several days to clear the great trunks that lay scattered across the tarmac like so many sticks in a fire grate. Most of the uprooted trees have long been cleared away, but the many newly planted woodlands bear silent testimony to the destruction of that savage October night.*

*Our walk begins with a piece of more ancient history, gazing up at the imposing bronze statue of King Alfred that dominates the eastern end of Winchester's Broadway. A plaque on the statue's massive granite base records that it was raised in September 1901 – and, though scholars now argue about the great King's dates, it's nice to imagine that Alfred's likeness **was** set up just a thousand years after his death in October 901.*

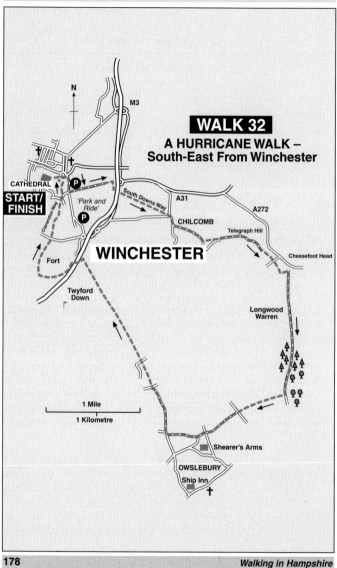

N

M3

WALK 32

**A HURRICANE WALK –
South-East From Winchester**

CATHEDRAL

**START/
FINISH**

*'Park and
Ride'*

South Downs Way

A31

A272

CHILCOMB

Telegraph Hill

Cheesefoot Head

WINCHESTER

Fort

Twyford
Down

Longwood
Warren

1 Mile

1 Kilometre

Shearer's Arms

OWSLEBURY

Ship Inn

Walk east from Alfred's statue, straight down the short High Street. The National Trust's City Mill is on our left as we cross the City Bridge and, in 50 yards, we swing right into Chesil Street. A further 300 yards brings us to the crossroads with Wharf Hill and East Hill; we turn left here, and follow East Hill for 50 yards before forking right into Petersfield Road. Pass All Saints church, built in the closing years of the nineteenth century to serve the new suburb of Highcliffe, and keep to the left-hand fork. Now we climb gently through a tree-lined avenue with a rash of expensive, newly built houses keeping us company on the left-hand side. At length Chalk Ridge swings off to the left and the road peters out, continuing as a tarmac footpath straight ahead. Here, the first **South Downs Way** sign – 'Eastbourne 100 miles' – points ambivalently over a chain-link fence. We ignore it, and turn hard right, with the unseen M3 motorway on our left. Soon we reach a children's play area on the right, and our path swings to the left over a motorway footbridge.

On the far side of the bridge we zigzag left and right, and head out into open country. Here, a wooden footpath sign points our way along the side of an open field, and the wire fence on our left is soon replaced by a tall, thickset hedge. In just over half a mile the path ends at a stile, where a backward glance is rewarded by views of some of Winchester's less distinguished buildings: the square police HQ, the Victorian prison, and the sprawling County Hospital.

Nip over the stile and bear half-left, signposted towards St Andrews church. The road swings right, passing Manor Farm and the attractive red-brick Manor House, and we follow it as it veers back to the left, where the road to the church forks off to the right. Now the road climbs away from the village, wriggling up through a wooded cutting and passing Hill Acre on the left. A hundred yards further on, a little wooden footpath sign points our way to the left up an inviting sunken path through the woods.

The path soon emerges from the woods, and we cross an open field with wide views to the left. After 100 yards we reach the gates on the far side of the field, and keep straight ahead onto a broad bridleway. A small conifer wood borders the right-hand side of the track as we climb towards the tumulus on **Telegraph Hill** and snake away through oddments of woodland towards **Cheesefoot Head**.

There are long views on either hand as another bridleway crosses our route; 100 yards further on, zigzag right and left through a scrappy hedge and wire fence before taking a hard left turn towards the A272 at a wooden bridleway signpost. The path climbs briefly towards a prominent green fertiliser tank on the skyline.

Here we turn right at the three-way bridleway sign, and follow the path as it heads across open fields for the short but muddy mile to Old Down plantation. Old Down is one of the many local woods that was flattened by the 1987 hurricane. Now cleared and replanted, the young trees at first nuzzle up on the right, finally enclosing the path on both sides as we pass through the blue metal field gates.

Enjoy a few hundred yards of easy walking on the hard forest track, before it swings away to the left at a three-way bridleway sign. Our way now lies straight ahead down a narrow woodland edge path which drops gently down to a bridleway 'crossroads' underneath an electricity power line. Here we turn right onto Honeyman Lane, a muddy track that picks its way between the rough thicket hedges and old coppice on either hand.

In just over half a mile we cross the Morestead Road at Bottom Pond Farm, continuing straight ahead onto the altogether different Stags Lane. This is easier walking, green underfoot and with low young hedges guarding the fields that rise gently away on either side. The short half mile to Jackman's Hill soon passes.

We're now in the parish of **Owslebury**, pronounced 'Uzzlebury' by the locals. *King Edgar had granted the land to the Bishop of Winchester in AD964 and, according to Domesday Book, the Bishop continued to hold it after the Norman Conquest. Later, it passed to the Seymour family of nearby Marwell Hall where, according to tradition, King Henry VIII came a-courting Lady Jane Seymour.*

If you feel like a break, we could turn left up Jackman's Hill and make the short 150 yard diversion to the **Shearer's Arms**. Otherwise, zigzag right and left, continuing up the narrow metalled lane that runs alongside the little brick and flint cottage numbered 43.

We keep to the right-hand fork at Mapledown Farm, and follow the lane to its junction with Mare Lane. Here we turn right and coast down the hill, crossing the Hazeley Road with a right and left zigzag and joining the bridleway that lifts us between wire fences across the grazing fields of Hazeley Down. Beyond the fields we pass through a metal gate and follow the path through a thin belt of trees to a second gate, where we zigzag over a farm track and continue with a hedge on our left and an open field on the right.

Half a mile further on we're joined by a wire fence on the right; soon we drop steeply down, cross a bridleway in the valley bottom, and begin the climb up onto **Twyford Down**, with the Hockley golf course on the left. On the crest of the hill Winchester heaves up over the skyline, and there are good views of the cathedral almost straight ahead. At the far corner of the golf course our wide green way again runs between wire fences, as far as the stile and wooden field gate that lead us into St Catherine's Hill nature reserve.

Few people can be unaware of the protracted struggle between the Department of Transport and the environmentalists who fought so hard to save this area from the M3 extension around Winchester. This hideous scar has eliminated the Hockley traffic lights with their notorious traffic jams – but similar queues are now a routine feature of the various approaches to junction 9, a couple of miles further north.

Over to our left a rough-hewn stone pillar overlooks the vast motorway cutting. Its simple inscription records that 'This land was ravaged by G. Malone, J. MacGregor, R. Key, J. Major, D. Keep, C. Parkinson, C. Patten, M. Thatcher, C. Chope'.

Continue straight ahead and follow the path down to the M3 foot-bridge; turn left across the motorway, and plunge back into the nature reserve beyond the wooden gate on the far side of the bridge. The obvious path leads us briefly down through the woods before settling into a gentle right-hand curve through the Plague Pits valley, last resting place for the victims of the Winchester Plague in 1666. On our right, the fortified bulk of St Catherine's Hill is, by tradition, the birthplace of the City of Winchester.

At the foot of the valley, two wooden gates in quick succession lead us out of the nature reserve and onto the towpath of the Itchen Navigation. We turn right here, and follow the path as far as the little car park at Tun Bridge, where we zigzag left and right over the old canal. Now on the opposite bank, we follow the Navigation for a further half mile, recrossing the water at Wharf Bridge and emerging through a small wicket gate onto an unmade road.

Turn left here, then bear right into Wharf Hill and, 100 yards further on, drop down to the left by the little green. Keep left around the front of Wharf Mill and cross the river once again, before turning right and following the tarmac path through the riverside gardens to the Old Monk pub and City Bridge. Turn left for the short 100 yard stroll back to our starting point at King Alfred's statue.

Long Distance Paths

Hampshire is fortunate in having a good choice of long distance paths which take walkers to the heart of the county. Only by exploring on foot can we appreciate Hampshire's gentle beauty and unique character. Over the years Hampshire County Council has developed an impressive network of trails that reaches into almost every corner of the county – from the rolling, windswept downland of its border country to the gleaming mudflats and military defences of the south coast. Many of the walks featured in this book coincide with stretches of these long distance routes.

The **Wayfarer's Walk**, which dates back to 1981, is one of Hampshire's most attractive trails. Extending the length of the county, from the mudflats of Chichester Harbour to the county boundary with Berkshire, this 70 mile route offers a constantly changing backdrop of varied scenery. Among the highlights en route are the delightful little town of Alresford, home of the Watercress steam railway, and the picturesque village of Droxford where Izaak Walton fished and the D-Day invasion plan was finalised.

The **Hangers Way** is a 21 mile trail linking Alton with the Queen Elizabeth Country Park on the western edge of the South Downs. The word 'hanger' is derived from the old English 'Hangra', meaning a wooded slope, and the path takes walkers to the heart of this glorious, beech-clad corner of East Hampshire – often called 'Little Switzerland'. The Hangers Way is well waymarked and, during the summer months, can be completed in a day. However, it would be a pity to rush it as there is plenty to capture our attention. Look out for deer, pheasants, woodpeckers and grey partridges. Jane Austen lived at nearby Chawton and knew the area well.

The **Clarendon Way** is 26 miles long and another of Hampshire County Council's regional routes, linking Winchester and Salisbury. The path takes its name from Clarendon Palace, a hunting lodge for Norman kings in Wiltshire. The guidebook describes the route as 'running across high land via long forgotten rideway routes, through old forests that echo with the creaking of Roman waggons and the cries of kings and their kingsmen in pursuit of deer'.

The **Test Way**, the third long distance trail created by Hampshire County Council, runs for 46 miles, beginning at Inkpen Beacon on the Berkshire border and finishing at Totton, near Southampton. Not surprisingly, the route follows the river valley for much of its length, starting high on the chalk downland where the pure, clear waters begin their journey underground. Part of the walk follows the trackbed of a disused railway line which, unusually, was built on the bed of an old canal linking Andover and Southampton.

The **Solent Way** is one of Hampshire's most spectacular trails. Beginning at Milford-on-Sea, on the edge of the New Forest, this 60 mile path begins by taking walkers along a pebble spit to Hurst Castle, built by Henry VIII to defend the western entrance to the Solent. From here the trail heads for Lymington and then inland, plunging deep into the New Forest. Beyond Southampton the walk follows the edge of Southampton Water, making for Netley, Hamble, Gosport and Portsmouth before finishing at Emsworth, overlooking Chichester Harbour.

The **South Downs Way**, one of our foremost national trails, is 90 miles long and links Winchester with Eastbourne. The trail runs like a thread across the ridge of the downs, providing a unique insight into some of the finest walking country in the south of England.

The **Staunton Way** extends for 12 miles between the Queen Elizabeth Country Park and the landscaped gardens of Staunton Country Park. Along the way it visits the villages of Chalton, Finchdean and Rowland's Castle and passes along the edge of Stansted Forest where Richard the Lionheart once hunted.

The **Avon Valley Path** follows the picturesque river valley from Christchurch to Salisbury and is 34 miles long. The trail runs along the western edge of the New Forest.

The **Pilgrims' Trail** is Hampshire's latest long distance trail and perhaps one of its more unusual. An ancient cross-Channel pilgrimage route forgotten for 400 years, the 155 mile trail begins at the shrine of St Swithun in Winchester Cathedral and finishes at Mont St Michel in Normandy. The Hampshire section runs through Bishop's Waltham and Southwick before heading for the ferry at Portsmouth.

Bibliography

The Beast and the Monk
  by Susan Chitty
  Hodder & Stoughton, 1974

Charles Kingsley: His letters and memories of his life (Volume 2)
  King & Co, 1877

Hampshire
  by J Charles Cox, revised by R L P Jowett
  Methuen, 1949

Hampshire
  by Adrian Rance
  Shire Publications, 1988

Hampshire Curiosities
  by Jo Draper
  The Dovecote Press, 1989

Hampshire Harvest
  by Robert Potter
  Phillimore, 1984

Hampshire Railways Remembered
  by Kevin Robertson & Leslie Oppitz
  Countryside Books, 1988

Hampshire Treasures
  Hampshire County Council, 1979

The Hampshire Village Book
  by Anthony Brode
  Countryside Books, 1988 edition

Hidden Hampshire
  by John Barton
  Countryside Books, 1989

History of the Great Western Railway (Volume 2)
  by MacDermot and Clinker
  Ian Allan, 1964

A History of the Southern Railway
  by C F Dendy Marshall
  Southern Railway Co, 1936

A History of the Worthy Villages
  Edited by Peter Finn & Pamela Johnston
  Worthys Local History Group, 1999

The Itchen Navigation
  by Edwin Course
  Southampton University, 1983

The King's England: Hampshire with the Isle of Wight
  by Arthur Mee
  Hodder and Stoughton, 1939

Lymington and Pennington Official Guide
  The British Publishing Co

The Mid-Hants Watercress Line – A Brief History
  Compiled by Charles Lewis
  Mid Hants Railway, 1980

The Nature of Hampshire and the Isle of Wight
  by Peter Brough, Bob Gibbons & Colin Pope
  Barracuda Books, 1986

Philip's County Guide: Hampshire
  General editor: Robin Dewhurst
  Text and maps: George Philip
  George Philip, 1993

Pub Walks for the Family: Hampshire and the New Forest
  by Nick Channer
  Countryside Books, 1994

The Visitor's Guide to Hampshire and the Isle of Wight
  by John Barton
  Moorland Publishing Co, 1985

Wayfarer's Walk
  by Linda Herbst, John Cann & Roger Lambert
  Hampshire County Recreation, 1988

CICERONE GUIDES

THE MIDLANDS

CANAL WALKS Vol: 2 Midlands   *Dennis Needham*
   ISBN 1 85284 225 3 176pp

TWENTY COTSWOLD TOWNS   *Clive Holmes*
   Clive describes and draws the most interesting features of these attractive towns.
   ISBN 1 85284 249 0 144pp A4 Case bound

THE COTSWOLD WAY   *Kev Reynolds*
   A glorious walk of 102 miles along high scarp edges, through woodlands and magical villages by
   one of Britain's best guide writers.
   ISBN 1 85284 049 8 168pp

COTSWOLD WALKS (3 volumes)   *Clive Holmes*
   60 walks of between 1 and 10 miles, with local points of interest explained. Beautifully illustrated.
   ISBN 1 85284 139 7 (North) 144pp
   ISBN 1 85284 140 0 (Central) 160pp
   ISBN 1 85284 141 9 (South) 144pp

THE GRAND UNION CANAL WALK   *Clive Holmes*
   13 easy stages along the canal which links the Black Country to London. Delightful illustrations.
   ISBN 1 85284 206 7 128pp

AN OXBRIDGE WALK   *J.A. Lyons*
   Over 100 miles linking the university cities of Oxford and Cambridge. Generally undemanding and
   easy to follow.
   ISBN 1 85284 166 4 168pp

WALKING IN OXFORDSHIRE   *Leslie Tomlinson*
   36 walks from all parts of the county, and suitable for all the family.
   ISBN 1 85284 244 X 200pp

WALKING IN WARWICKSHIRE   *Brian Conduit*
   Attractive pastoral and gentle hill walks include Shakespeare country, the Avon and the Stour.
   Features many historic villages.
   ISBN 1 85284 255 5 136pp

WALKING IN WORCESTERSHIRE   *David Hunter*
   Part of the ever growing County Series, this book describes walks for all the family in
   Worcestershire.
   ISBN 1 85284 286 5 200pp 9

WEST MIDLANDS ROCK   *Doug Kerr*
   A guide to the popular crags.
   ISBN 1 85284 200 8 168pp

SOUTH AND SOUTH-WEST LONG DISTANCE TRAILS

THE KENNET & AVON WALK   *Ray Quinlan*
   90 miles along riverside and canal, from Westminster to Avonmouth, full of history, wildlife, delec-
   table villages and pubs.
   ISBN 1 85284 090 0 200pp

THE LEA VALLEY WALK   *Leigh Hatts*
   Split into 20 stages this 50 mile walk is one of the finest and most varied walking routes around the
   capital, tracing the route of the River Lea from the Millennium Dome to its source.
   ISBN 1 85284 313 6 128pp)

THE NORTH DOWNS WAY and THE SOUTH DOWNS WAY   *Kev Reynolds*
Two major walks. The North Downs Way runs west from Farnham to Dover, while the South Downs way is a glorious easterly walk from Eastbourne. The routes are each split into 12 day sections, with advice on stopping points.

THE SOUTHERN COAST-TO-COAST WALK   *Ray Quinlan*
The equivalent of the popular northern walk. 283 miles from Weston-super-Mare to Dover.
ISBN 1 85284 117 6 200pp

SOUTH WEST WAY - A Walker's Guide to the Coast Path   *Martin Collins*
Vol.1: Minehead to Penzance
ISBN 1 85284 025 0 184pp PVC cover

Vol.2: Penzance to Poole
ISBN 1 85284 026 9 198pp PVC cover
Two volumes which cover the spectacular 560 mile coastal path around Britain's south-west peninsula. Profusely illustrated and filled with practical details.

THE THAMES PATH   *Leigh Hatts*
From the Thames Barrier to the source. This popular guide provides all the information needed to complete this delightful scenic route. 180 miles in 20 stages.
ISBN 1 85284 270 9 184pp

THE TWO MOORS WAY   *James Roberts*
100 miles crossing Dartmoor the delightful villages of central Devon and Exmoor to the rugged coast at Lynmouth.
ISBN 1 85284 159 1 100pp £5.99

THE WEALDWAY AND THE VANGUARD WAY   *Kev Reynolds*
Two long distance walks, from the outskirts of London to the south coast. The 81 mile Wealdway runs from Gravesend to Beachy Head, while the 62 mile Vanguard Way goes from Croydon to Seaford Head in Sussex.
ISBN 0 902363 85 9 160pp

SOUTHERN AND SOUTH-EAST ENGLAND

CANAL WALKS Vol 3: South   *Dennis Needham*
ISBN 1 85284 227 X 176pp

WALKING IN BUCKINGHAMSHIRE   *Robert Wilson*
32 walks through bluebell woods, rolling Chiltern hills and pretty villages. The walks are of short and medium length for all abilities and interests, including sections of Icknield Way.
ISBN 1 85284 301 2)

WALKING IN THE CHILTERNS   *Duncan Unsworth*
35 short circular walks in this area of woods and little valleys with cosy pubs and old churches.
ISBN 1 85284 127 3 184pp

WALKING IN BEDFORDSHIRE   *Alan Castle*
32 fascinating walks of short and medium length for all abilities and interests. Maps and details of local interest abound.
ISBN 1 85284 312 8

A WALKER'S GUIDE TO THE ISLE OF WIGHT   *Martin Collins & Norman Birch*
The best walks on this sunshine island, including short circuits and longer trails.
ISBN 1 85284 221 0 216 pp

WALKING IN KENT: Vol I   *Kev Reynolds*
ISBN 1 85284 192 3 200pp

WALKING IN KENT: Vol II *Kev Reynolds*
ISBN 1 85284 156 7 200pp
Two books which cover the best of walking in the county.

LONDON THEME WALKS *Frank Duerden*
Ten fascinating walks based on popular themes.
ISBN 1 85284 145 1 144pp

RURAL RIDES No.1: WEST SURREY
ISBN 1 85284 272 5 192pp

RURAL RIDES No.2: EAST SURREY
ISBN 1 85284 273 3 160pp *Ron Strutt*

WALKING IN SUSSEX *Kev Reynolds*
40 walks in the great variety of scenery and history of Sussex. Short walks and more demanding routes, including outline descriptions of some of the region's long distance paths.
ISBN 1 85284 292 X 240pp

SOUTH-WEST ENGLAND

CHANNEL ISLAND WALKS *Paddy Dillon*
47 one-day walks in this wonderful holiday area, with easy bus and boat services. Walks on Jersey, Guernsey, Alderney, Sark and Herm.
ISBN 1 85284 288 1

CORNISH ROCK *Rowland Edwards & Tim Dennell*
A superb photo topo guide to West Penwith, the most popular climbing in Cornwall, by the area's leading activists.
ISBN 1 85284 208 3 234pp A5 size Casebound

WALKING IN CORNWALL *John Earle*
30 walks including the Coast Path and the interesting interior.
ISBN 1 85284 217 2 200pp

WALKING ON DARTMOOR *John Earle*
The most comprehensive walking guide to the National Park. Includes 43 walks and outlines 4 longer walks.
ISBN 0 902363 84 0 224pp

WALKING IN DEVON *David Woodthorpe*
16 coastal, 15 countryside and 14 Dartmoor walks.
ISBN 1 85284 223 7 200pp

WALKING IN DORSET *James Roberts*
Circular walks between 5 and 12 miles in a rich variety of scene. Spectacular coastline, lovely downs and fine pubs.
ISBN 1 85284 180 X 232pp

A WALKER'S GUIDE TO THE PUBS OF DARTMOOR *Chris Wilson & Michael Bennie*
60 Dartmoor inns. Everything a walker needs to know.
ISBN 1 85284 115 X 152 pp

EXMOOR AND THE QUANTOCKS *John Earle*
Walks for all the family on the moors, valleys and coastline.
ISBN 1 85284 083 8 200pp

WALKING IN THE ISLES OF SCILLY *Paddy Dillon*
With its mild climate and relaxing atmosphere, this is an ideal retreat. Walks and boat trips are described, with stunning scenery and beautiful plants and flowers.
ISBN 1 85284 310 1